D1348789

The Kirk and the Kingdom

A Century of Tension in Scottish Social Theology,
1830–1929

The Chalmers Lectures for 2011

Johnston McKay

Edinburgh University Press

For Evelyn and Cally

© Johnston McKay, 2012

Edinburgh University Press Ltd
22 George Square, Edinburgh
www.euppublishing.com

Typeset in Sabon by
3btype.com, and
printed and bound in Great Britain by
CPI Group (UK) Ltd, Croydon CR0 4YY

A CIP record for this book is available from the British Library

ISBN 978 0 7486 4473 5 (hardback)

Contents

Acknowledgements

I am extremely grateful to the Trustees of the Chalmers Lectureship for the invitation to deliver the 2011 Chalmers Lectures on which this book is based. The Chalmers Lectures are always connected to 'The Headship of Christ over the Church'. I must also thank the Baird Trust and the Hope Trust for their financial assistance in the publication of this book.

In the preparation of the lectures and this book I have benefited enormously from being a Visiting Fellow of New College in Edinburgh during 2010 and 2011. I am hugely grateful to the New College authorities for granting me the fellowship. The staff of New College Library, the National Library of Scotland, Scotland's National Archive and the Mitchell Library in Glasgow have given sympathetic and remarkably tolerant understanding to much pestering by e-mail from the Ayrshire coast. I have also been able to stay in Edinburgh for extended periods thanks to the hospitality of Canonmills Baptist Church in allowing preachers from beyond the city and its neighbourhood to live in the manse. When Dr Alison Elliot was elected Moderator of the General Assembly of the Church of Scotland in 2004, I was delighted to be asked to be one of her chaplains. Any help I was able to give her during that year has been more than amply repaid by the wise comments she has made and the sound advice she has given as this book went through its various stages. The friendship of Alison and her husband Jo, along with all I owe to New College, have combined to dissolve the congenital suspicion of the capital city of a proud son of the west coast.

I must acknowledge other personal debts: to Professor S. J. Brown of New College for his unfailing interest and encouragement; to two friends, the late Professors Alec Cheyne and John O'Neill, inspiring examples of scholarship at its best, whose deaths deprived me of their wisdom and advice; to Lily Buntain, who read the manuscript and made helpful suggestions; to my son Robert who gave word-processing assistance at crucial crisis moments in preparing the book for publication; to John Watson and the staff of Edinburgh University Press who made the production of *The Kirk and the Kingdom* far less daunting that it would otherwise have been; but most of all to my wife Evelyn and daughter Cally for all they mean to me and do for me. While I very willingly acknowledge all these debts, the responsibility for the content of this book is, of course, entirely mine.

Johnston McKay

Introduction

In a famous and frequently quoted altercation between Andrew Melville and King James VI, Melville said:

> And thairfor, Sir, as divers tymes before, sa now again, I mon tell yow, thair is twa Kings and twa Kingdoms in Scotland. Thair is Chryst Jesus the King and his kingdome the Kirk, whase subject King James the saxt is, and of whase kingdome nocht a king, nor a lord, nor a heid, bot a member! And they whome Christ hes callit and commandit to watch over his Kirk, and governe his spiritual kingdome, hes sufficient powar of him, and authorities sa to do, bathe togidder and severalie; the quhilk na Christian King nor Prince sould control and discharge, but fortify and assist, utherwayes nocht faithfull subjects nor members of Christ.[1]

In this Melville was following John Calvin, who had taught that the petition in the Lord's Prayer 'Thy Kingdom come' should not be taken to imply that it did not exist already, because God has reigned from the beginning of time. The Kingdom exists already in the company of the elect.[2]

The argument of this study is that until the second half of the nineteenth century in Scotland, the Kingdom and the Kirk were regarded as identical: not totally, because there was always an understanding of the Kingdom that lay in the future, realised in God's own time. However, that the Kingdom and the Kirk were in some identical relationship such as Melville described to James VI was not in doubt.

What was also not in doubt was that if the poorest and most deprived were to escape from poverty and deprivation, the only route open to them was through the Church. Of course it took some time for the Church in Scotland to abandon the conviction, which it expressed powerfully in the metrical version of Psalm 148:

> From God your beings are
> him therefore famous make;
> you all created were,
> when he the word but spake.
>
> > And from that place
> > where fixed you be
> > by his decree
> > you cannot pass

Thomas Chalmers certainly believed that the class structure of society was divinely authorised and that the economic structure of the nation was dictated by the operation of natural forces. However he supported the alleviation of poverty and a better standard of living for the poor, though he was not convinced that poverty was as extensive as was thought:

> The truth is, that there is a far greater sufficiency among the lower classes of society than is generally imagined, and our first impressions of their want and wretchedness are generally by too much aggravated; nor do we know a more effectual method of reducing these impressions than to cultivate a closer acquaintance with their resources, and their habits.[3]

Chalmers did not accept that poverty could or should be alleviated by political change in or economic intervention by the state. If, however, those in extreme poverty underwent moral and personal change then there would be no improvement in their condition that would be impossible to achieve. It was only through the Church that Chalmers believed people could bring about 'a moral and personal change upon themselves', and his policy of subdividing parishes in industrial Scotland and providing each divided parish with a church of its own, with patrons taking note of popular opinion in the appointment of ministers, was, as far as Chalmers was concerned, the only way to overcome deprivation and poverty, whose root causes, he believed, lay in the lack of religious faith and commitment.

It took the Church in Scotland a long time to shake off the view that if there were structural causes of poverty and deprivation they had God's sanction, and that the only way to escape poor social conditions was through faith in God and commitment to the Church. The years of the nineteenth century when Chalmers' views were widely shared have been characterised as years of complacency and passive obedience. This judgement is unfair, however. This study will ask if it is any more accurate to describe the Paisley radical Patrick Brewster as 'the unique exception' to a culture of complacency[4] and to regard Norman Macleod of the Barony in Glasgow as the proponent of a new theology[5] than it is to ignore the social and practical theology of their contemporaries and neighbours Robert Burns in Paisley and Robert Buchanan in Glasgow. These four nineteenth-century Scottish churchmen had no other vehicle for the expression of their social concern than their shared assumption that social reform could only come about as people were encouraged out of poverty through the life of the Church. There was no other model available to them until a young, relatively unknown minister in Aberdeen's East Church preached a series of sermons on weeknight evenings in 1859. He was Robert Flint, and when these sermons were published six years later,[6] they offered the Church an alternative to social reform through the Church. Flint argued that the

Church should not be confused with the Kingdom of God, for the Kingdom of God included far more than the Church, and its coming would be advanced by other individuals and institutions than the ecclesiastical. It was this insight that greatly influenced men in the Church of Scotland like Donald Macleod and John Marshall Lang, who have been credited with making the case for the Church's engagement with society. On the other hand, the Glasgow minister Frederick Lockhart Robertson has gone unrecognised, despite playing a major part in the setting up of the Church of Scotland Presbytery of Glasgow's Housing Commission and single-handed promoting a far wider support for its conclusions. Within the United Free Church of Scotland, Flint's view that Kingdom and Church were not identical became commonplace, but what the Church's specific contribution should be to the coming of the Kingdom was the subject of often acrimonious debate.

In the years covered by this study there were three different understandings of the Kingdom of God and Jesus' preaching of it, though authors sometimes slipped from one to the other without apparently realising they were doing so. They were reflected powerfully in the hymns people sang in church. One view regarded the Kingdom of God as the earthly ordering of things by humans based on the universal recognition of the reign of Christ. This view saw the Kingdom as a distant objective which could only be realised in the future since it had to be implemented throughout the world, but it was believed the Kingdom would gradually advance to its fulfilment on earth:

> Rise up, O men of God
> His Kingdom tarries long;
> Bring in the day of brotherhood
> And end the night of wrong.

A second view understood the Kingdom of God to be a spiritual dynamic where the Kingdom existed in the hearts of its citizens rather than in the objective world of events. It would result eventually in transforming the life of the world through the transformation of individuals:

> Let thy Kingdom come, we pray thee;
> Let the world in thee find rest;
> Let all know thee, and obey thee,
> Loving, praising, blessing, blest.

A third view was that the Kingdom would come through a supernatural event, which it was beyond any human agency to influence:

Thy Kingdom come, O God,
Thy rule, O Christ, begin;
Break with thine iron rod,
The tyrannies of sin.

This study traces the interplay between these views of the Kingdom of God. The Kingdom of God was the context in which those who held very different attitudes towards the Church's engagement with society argued for which role the Church should take in the political, social and economic issues facing society. Gradually, the view that the Church's role in advancing the Kingdom should be an inspirational rather than a politically and socially active one gained acceptance, and Flint's vision of the Kingdom of Christ upon earth, which was brought closer through the Church's cooperation with secular agencies, faded into the background. The emergence of social criticism and theology within the uniting Presbyterian churches in Scotland was regarded as of less importance than purely ecclesiastical concerns.

NOTES

1. Pitcairn, R. (1842) *The Autobiography and Diary of Mr James Melvill* (Edinburgh: Woodrow Society), p. 370.
2. Calvin, John (1837) *Calvin's Tracts and Treatises in Defence of the Reformed Faith*, vol. 3 (trans. H. Beveridge) (Edinburgh: Oliver and Boyd).
3. Chalmers, T. (1856) *Select Works*, vol. X (Edinburgh: Thomas Constable & Son), p. 168.
4. Smith, Donald (1987) *Passive Obedience and Prophetic Protest* (New York: Peter Lang), p. 175ff.
5. Hillis, Peter (1992) 'Towards a new social theology; the contribution of Norman Macleod', *Records of the Scottish Church History Society*, vol. XXIV, pp. 263–85.
6. Flint, Robert (1865) *Christ's Kingdom upon Earth* (Edinburgh: William Blackwood & Sons).

1

Signs and Signals

The Stirrings of Social Criticism

> There is something wrong in the structure of society, and in the laws which regulate the intercourse of nations.
>
> Revd Dr Robert Burns, 1841

There was nowhere more hungry at the beginning of the hungry forties than the town of Paisley, the fifth-largest town in Scotland. In the previous twenty years its population had risen by almost 30 per cent to over 60,000, putting an impossible strain on the system of poor relief when the local economy took a downturn, which it had been threatening to do from 1837 and did dramatically in 1841. Sixty-seven out of one hundred and twelve merchant and manufacturing firms failed. Weavers looked to Friendly Societies in times of hardship, but in 1841 almost half of the Friendly Societies collapsed. In the winter of 1841–2, 15,000 men, representing well over 25 per cent of the town's population, were considered destitute. A deputation of civic leaders, led by Provost John Henderson, who was editor of a Chartist newspaper, *The Glasgow Post and Reformer*, and the Revd Dr Robert Burns, minister of St George's Church in the town, travelled to London and met members of the government: the Prime Minister, Sir Robert Peel; the Home Secretary, Sir James Graham; and Lord Stanley, the Colonial Secretary. According to Peel's biographer Douglas Hurd, this meeting 'lodged Paisley in the mind of ministers'.[1] The number of the town's destitute had risen by 2,000. By March the Kirk sent a Memorial to the government, reinforcing conditions in Paisley in the Prime Minister's mind: 'There is a general feeling of deep and settled discontent. Hopeless and worn out with either continued depression or often recurring distress, many have lost much of their wanted self-respect. Their homes are sometimes the picture of extreme wretchedness.'[2] In July a further Memorial was sent to the Home Secretary from the Presbytery of Paisley but clearly organised and drafted by Burns and supported by ministers from other denominations in the town. It outlined the recent history of distress in the town, referred to its causes both national and local, and suggested remedies which, it was believed, would alleviate the situation. The Presbytery was 'under the painful feeling that if matters were allowed to go on as they have been for a number of years past, consequences more dreadful than any which have yet appeared will manifestly ensue'.[3]

Peel began to raise money for Paisley. The three government ministers who had met the delegation from Paisley each contributed £225. Peel persuaded the Queen and the Marquess of Abercorn each to give £500. Sir James Graham went to the London Manufacturers' Relief Committee, which had been set up to meet similar needs in England in the 1820s, and secured a gift of £12,500. Peel then prevailed on the Queen to write an open letter to be read in churches throughout the country, asking for support for Paisley. Eventually a Relief Committee for Paisley, chaired by Provost John Henderson, was set up which supported destitute families with both meal tickets and money. One third of all the sums raised nationally for the destitute was earmarked for Paisley. It was to be many years before it became clear that counteracting poverty at the level it existed in Paisley was far beyond the capacity of such philanthropic efforts, but in terms of the thinking of the day, the deputation to the government in which Dr Robert Burns played a leading part, and the pressure which he made sure was continued, had a considerable effect on welfare provision in the town.

REVD DR ROBERT BURNS

Robert Burns was only twenty-two when he arrived in Paisley in 1818, defeating three more senior candidates for presentation by the Town Council to the charge of the Laigh Kirk. Despite his youthful appearance he was said to display an almost premature ripeness and maturity in theology. Burns had been educated at the University of Edinburgh and was sufficiently intellectually able to be considered by supporters as a possible applicant in 1823 for the Chair of Moral Philosophy in St Andrews when Thomas Chalmers was appointed. Within ten years of Burns' induction, a large church, given the name of St George's, had to be built nearby to accommodate the greatly increased congregation which had been built up.

Shortly after he went to Paisley, Burns published a painstaking examination of how the Poor Law operated.[4] Until 1845, when the Poor Law Act was passed, support for the poor was provided by the Heritors (the landowners who were obliged to maintain parish churches, pay ministers and also provide funds for the poor) and Kirk Sessions who largely relied on voluntary contributions from those attending church, and from any funds specifically set aside for the purpose. There was no obligation to provide support for those who were able-bodied or who had not lived within the parish for some time. At a time of mass unemployment and migration, these restrictions resulted in an ineffective Poor Law system, and the funds available to the Church as a whole were woefully inadequate to cope with urban poverty. Throughout the nineteenth century, opinion was sharply divided. There were those who continued to believe that the existing voluntary system was both desirable in itself and capable of being revitalised to meet the challenge of an urban environment. Meanwhile, those who supported Dr William Alison's conviction that a voluntary system of parochial poor relief may have suited when Scotland was made up largely of rural communities, but was incapable of dealing with an urban, industrial society, believed that there required to be a legally enforceable system of poor relief levied on local communities.

Burns' *Dissertations* were prompted by his dissatisfaction with a report that the General Assembly of the Church of Scotland had been asked to produce for parliament on the working of the Poor Law generally, and in particular whether the assessment on Heritors was likely to become excessive. This report was drawn up on the basis of a questionnaire sent to all parish ministers, and Burns maintained that the questions put were so imprecise that answers could not properly be compiled, that the returns from ministers had been inaccurately recorded and that the arithmetic was 'in numberless instances' inaccurate, with the result that 'the entire report was flawed'. For example, in contrast to the report's recording of the population of Paisley as 19,937, Burns carefully argued for a figure of 45,000, a difference of 25,000, and subjected the returns for other areas to similar close examination. In terms of policy, Burns argued against making assessments on Heritors legally enforceable. He believed that to do so would encourage the view that support for the poor was an entitlement, which in turn would encourage dependence and so mask the difference between genuine need and personal fecklessness. The thoroughness of Burns' research, the strength of his arguments and the passion of his concern do not suggest any complacency about the problem of poverty.

Burns' parochial ministry in Paisley confirms his commitment to social issues, although he did write harshly that in the early years of his ministry he was disinclined 'to do anything at all, ecclesiastically, for benefiting the temporal interest of the working classes'. According to a biography of him written by his son, Burns was

all the time in the streets and lanes of the town on missions of benevolence. All the charitable institutions enjoyed his advocacy and felt his care. Connection with their boards was to him no mere sinecure. He was chairman of emigration societies to facilitate the exodus of the deserving poor to those lands of promise which Britain's colonies supplied.

There may be a hint of filial piety in the description of 'long rows of poverty-stricken people reaching from his study desk out into the street, eager to pour into his ready ear the story of their woes', but Burns' commitment to the poor was confirmed by Provost John Henderson:

> Dr Burns was something more than an eminent clergyman – he was in the truest and best sense of the word, a citizen of the town. He shrank from no labour, but threw himself with the whole force of his character into every good work. During his long residence among us there was no public question, no movement or organisation having for its object the social and political amelioration of the people, or the material, moral or spiritual wellbeing of the community which did not command and receive his eloquent advocacy and indefatigable working. There is one sphere of his labours on behalf of this community in connection with which I was perhaps more than any other brought into contact with him … My first connection with efforts for the relief of unemployed operatives was in 1837, and I well recollect the active labours of Dr Burns on that occasion; and on a similar state of matters in 1841 and 1842, it was my fortune to be associated with the Doctor as members of a deputation to London, to press the state of matters on the attention of the government, and to endeavour, by subscription, to raise money to relieve the starving population of this town, and I can never forget the herculean exertions which our friend put forth on that occasion.[5]

As Burns admitted, he had not always been of the view that a minister of the Kirk should become involved in politics. He wrote in some auto-biographical notes which his son quotes in his biography:

> When I first published my volume on the poor in 1818 I had by no means got above the dominant prejudice [against the Church's involvement in politics]. Circumstances connected with the depression of trade and with the civil disabilities which impeded the prosperity of Scotland gradually enlarged and liberalised my views, and during the second half of the period of my ministry in Scotland, I not only felt and acted on the principle that the Church ought to *do more* than she had done for relief of the humbler classes, but I pleaded occasionally from the platform and from the press on behalf of the removal of iniquitous and oppressive laws, such as those which affected the importation of corn and provisions from foreign ports. With great difficulty did I obtain a scrimp majority of votes in our Presbytery for a searching enquiry into the causes of prevailing distress among the working classes of our community.[6]

The extent to which Burns changed his mind is obvious from three lectures which he delivered in Paisley in 1841 and 1842.[7] In the light of the conditions in the town, Burns became persuaded that the Christian minister must be involved in politics, though at the level of principle rather than party. He recognised the limitations of political involvement which, he says, could not regenerate humanity 'without the religious and moral means which God has been pleased to appoint', but 'the form of civil administration can dictate the extent to which these moral and religious influences will influence society', and so Christian ministers were bound to be concerned with civil administration. He described ministers who proudly claimed to be 'no politicians' as 'a disgrace' and believed the reason ministers and congregations of the Church of Scotland were so seldom seen to support political rights was that patronage, and what he regarded as its corrosive effect, had diminished political radicalism in the Church.

Burns continued to promote the need for an investigation both into the causes of a nation's prosperity and into the degree of distress there was among the poor as well as its causes. When such widespread poverty exists, 'the inference is that there is something wrong in the structure of society, and in the laws which regulate the intercourse of nations'. He was now convinced that there had to be public, legislative provision for the poor whose needs could not be met by private charity alone, though he did not think that public provision should be seen as a reason to remove the support of private charity. Without legislative provision for the poor there would be an inevitable and regrettable increase in begging. Public provision for the poor should not be restricted to the provision of food but should be made available for clothing and education also. Burns supported the establishment of a widespread programme of public works, though there is perhaps a degree of inconsistency between his support for public works and his belief that 'collecting the paupers in gangs for the performance of parish work is found to be more immediately injurious to their conduct than even allowance or relief without requiring work'.

Burns still regarded individual regeneration inspired by the Gospel as essential in bringing about social improvement, but he was not alone in that, and it is significant that as an evangelical, he saw a place for public funding to provide work. The decline of Paisley's economy and the consequent widespread distress had taught Burns that there was more to the causes of poverty than the moral failure of individuals.

REVD DR ROBERT BUCHANAN

There was more in Scotland to occupy the attention of the Church and the government in 1842 than poverty in Paisley. The Ten Years Conflict, which was to culminate in the Disruption and the creation of the Free Church of Scotland, which Robert Burns joined, was reaching its climax. The historian of the Ten Years Conflict from the Free Church standpoint was Robert Buchanan, who in 1833 became minister of Glasgow's Tron Parish, which included the notoriously deprived Wynds area, where those who had once worked in the declining weaving industry lived. According to one estimate, the average population per acre in Glasgow was 65 but in the Wynds area it was 583. Buchanan estimated the true population to be almost twice that figure. The conditions in Buchanan's parish were graphically described by Friedrich Engels in 1844:

> I have seen wretchedness in some of its worst phases, both here and on the Continent, but until I visited the wynds of Glasgow, I did not believe that so much crime, misery and disease could exist in any civilised country ... The wynds of Glasgow contain a fluctuating population of fifteen to thirty thousand human beings. This quarter consists wholly of narrow alleys and square courts, in the middle of every one of which there lies a dung heap. Revolting as was the outward appearance of these courts, I was yet not prepared for the filth and wretchedness within. In some of the sleeping places which we visited at night ... we found a complete layer of human beings stretched upon the floor, often fifteen to twenty, some clad, others naked, men and women indiscriminately. Their bed was a litter of mouldy straw, mixed with rags.[8]

Buchanan was heavily involved in the later stages of the Ten Years Conflict. He was one of the deputation sent to meet the Prime Minister, by then Lord Melbourne, to effect a reconciliation. Like many of his congregation in what became, after the Disruption, Tron Free Church, he moved to the west of the city to be minister of the Free College Church. For nearly thirty years Buchanan was the convener of the vitally important Sustentation Fund, to which all congregations contributed and from which the Free Kirk ministers drew their stipends. He was Moderator of the Free Church General Assembly in 1860 and died in 1875. His biographer noted that 'it was only after the excitement of the Disruption was over that he was able to address himself to that work in the Wynds in which he appeared most characteristically as the parochial minister'.[9] Buchanan himself acknowledged that what he encountered in the Wynds forced his mind to focus more clearly on social policy and social theology.

In a public lecture in 1850, in which he dealt with social policy and theology and argued for an increase in funds for educational provision, Buchanan said that conditions in the lanes and alleys of Glasgow had compelled men to open their ears to the cry of the social evils which had been growing unheeded.

Although Donald Smith admits that it would be 'wrong to suggest that the Church in Scotland in the 1830s and 40s was unaware of the social evils and problems which were manifesting themselves in industrial society', he levels a serious charge against the Church in Scotland in the middle years of the nineteenth century:

Being insufficiently alive to the radical nature of the changes taking place in the whole fabric of social life, whereby a simple, agrarian, paternalistic society was being rapidly transformed into a complex, competitive, industrial one, the Church merely stressed with renewed emphasis in these decades the traditional moral virtues and values which were largely meaningless in the industrial context. It simply tried to moralise all the new social and economic relations by treating each transaction as a case of personal conduct, involving personal responsibility. In this way even the most complex social evils of industrial society were reduced to a matter of personal morality.[10]

There is an element of truth in the charge, but not a sufficiently serious element to justify Smith's dismissive assessment. The Church was not alone in interpreting social ills in terms of individual morality, or the lack of it, and the approach of Robert Buchanan illustrates how difficult it is to make sweeping judgements even about the attitude of one particular churchman. Undoubtedly Buchanan made the typical contemporary judgement that poverty could be attributed to a failure in personal morality. 'Let anyone examine the rank and file of that huge army [of paupers] more than 70,000 strong, which has come like a cloud of locusts upon the city,' he wrote, 'and when he has told off all those whose pauperism can be traced, without effort, to idleness, improvidence and intemperance, there will be little more than the mere skeleton of the army left behind.'[11] However, in a speech to the Free Church's Glasgow Presbytery in January 1851, when he insisted that social questions were now the questions of the day, intemperance, pauperism and crime receive only a passing mention,[12] and in a subsequent pamphlet, they are referred to only to introduce the statistic that Glasgow spent £186,000 on pauperism and crime and only £36,000 on ministry and education.[13]

Buchanan's 1851 speech persuaded the Free Church Presbytery of Glasgow to present a proposal (formally called an 'overture') to the General Assembly on the issue of spiritual destitution. In presenting the overture to the Assembly, Buchanan described his parish area, which, he said, included 115 places for the sale of alcohol, 63 pawn shops and 33 brothels. He criticised those in other areas of the city, who neither knew nor cared how the poorer population lived and asked how the city benefited if its commercial success masked such widespread poverty. He recognised that the conditions in his parish were exactly those that fuelled revolutionary flames on the Continent and, as a solution, proposed 'the old specific of well-wrought territorial Churches and schools' but at the same time stating forcefully the case for the provision of day schools, libraries and savings banks. Although Buchanan reflected the common view which attributed poverty to moral failure, he was much more concerned to stress to the Church the consequences of poverty and to convince it that the Church, and to a certain extent society, had acquiesced in these. 'We have refused to spend money on reforming society,' he said. Unless society took measures to prevent poverty and pauperism, 'any thing like a real and lasting amelioration of the conditions of the poorer and most destitute classes of society may be regarded as hopeless'. In his parish, Buchanan was the driving force behind putting a schoolmaster in the Wynds. He raised funds to buy a candle factory and set up a system of educational visitors to provide schooling, encouraging parents who could pay for it to do so and relying on the support of patrons to provide for those parents who could not. He told the General Assembly of 1851,

> The men I especially plead for are the decent hard working men who live [in the Wynds] and yet are still uncontaminated. I plead for the men who, with every disadvantage, are endeavouring to prevent themselves and their families from sinking lower in the scale. I plead for the men, numbers of whom may, ere another session passes, be elevated to the position of electors for the position of members of Parliament, and who need to be qualified for their trust.[14]

Buchanan acknowledged in the second pamphlet he published in 1851 that what he saw in the Wynds forced him to see beyond ecclesiastical concerns:

> Providence often assigns to an individual a particular work in such a way as leaves him no room to escape from doing it … When I entered on the efforts which are now in progress in the Wynds, I had no thought of meddling with any further field. It was the discoveries made there that gradually forced upon me the general question of the state of the masses in the city at large.

Buchanan believed that the moral condition of society determined its economic prosperity, but that should not be construed as implying a lack of interest in improving the social conditions of the poorest in his parish.

He condemned class divisions, which he saw as very real. In his book *Schoolmaster in the Wynds* he drew a very unfavourable comparison between conditions in the deprived parish where he ministered in the Wynds and the comfortable areas like Garnethill and Blythswood to which the middle classes had moved, and which he described as 'socially as well as geographically one of the *higher* parts of the city'. He quoted a survey undertaken by the Town Council which showed that in 1841 the population of the Tron Parish was just over 10,000, 1,586 of whom were aged between 6 and 16, of whom only 567 attended school, whereas in Blythswood and Garnethill, with a similar size of population, there were 1,606 children between the ages of 6 and 16, 1,508 of whom attended school. It is fair to say that Buchanan regarded education as having a moral and spiritual purpose, but he consistently recognised that it also had a vital social function. The uneducated, he pointed out, were the first to experience unemployment in time of recession.

When he refers to those who are better off, Buchanan moves beyond comparison to criticism. In introducing the Presbytery's overture to the General Assembly of 1851, he contrasted the conditions of profligacy, filth and crime which resulted in wives and children who 'starve in rags and wretchedness in their miserable dwelling' with 'the amount of heartless selfishness and unthinking gaiety' of 'peoples, in other quarters of the city, its splendid streets and terraces and squares ... that neither knows nor cares how its poorer population lives'. This is not the language of someone uncritically acquiescing in the upward social mobility of those who had moved their homes west from the Tron parish, nor is it pandering to middle-class self-interest.

Like many of his day Buchanan believed that the political engagement which was required to bring about social improvement was not the business of the institutional Church, though by his 1851 speech he had abandoned an earlier conviction that social conditions would be improved mainly, if not solely, through the Church's mission and evangelism and its effect on individuals. As Callum Brown has argued, Buchanan went beyond seeing the territorial area as the focus for social reform and became 'the key inspiration to the mid-Victorian civic Gospel in Glasgow'. Brown regards Buchanan as 'inspiring the beginnings of mass-scale slum clearance in Britain' through a building society which would first buy and then demolish property, a move that eventually saw the passing of the 1866 City Improvement Act'.[15] Buchanan was involved in education, in a building society and in the Glasgow Relief Fund Committee. His ministry always had a social dimension. He wrote in his account of the educational work in the Wynds:

> The reformation of the masses is a subject that branches out into many wide and important details. Better dwellings for the working classes, the opening of new streets in dense and overcrowded districts, sanitary improvements, the state and working of the poor laws, and beyond and above all, these measures for ameliorating the physical condition of the people, the educating of the young, and the bringing of the hallowing influences and ordinances of religion to bear on even the poorest and most destitute of people. Here is one thing – a thing tangible and definite – and lying at the same time at the very bottom of the whole question of social improvement. Let this be taken up and grappled with on an adequate scale, grappled with by the Christian liberality and the Christian agency of the evangelical denominations of Glasgow, and it will draw a thousand other reformatory measures in its train.[16]

Robert Buchanan's approach to improving social conditions rested on two convictions which were widely shared: that the political activity required was not the business of the courts nor of the pulpits of the Church, and that the aggressive territorial ministry of Thomas Chalmers provided the best framework not only for evangelism but for improving social conditions. Buchanan was an evangelical who regarded evangelism as important for the tackling of poverty. This is something for which he was criticised for when he promoted the Glasgow Free Church Building Society. He was active in the Relief Fund Committee set up to respond to the 1847 potato famines in Ireland and the Highlands of Scotland. He visited and inspected the lodging houses of Glasgow's East End. He was a trustee of Anderson's University and Hutcheson's Hospital, both of which were specifically for the poor. He was also instrumental in establishing the first savings bank to accept deposits as low as one penny. Like others he saw poverty through an evangelical prism, but one that encouraged rather than distorted his keen social conscience.

REVD PATRICK BREWSTER

Patrick Brewster was the son of a Jedburgh headmaster and brother of the scientist Sir David Brewster. He became minister of the second charge of Paisley Abbey in 1828, and his ministry was uncontroversial, perhaps even mundane, until he made headlines in 1835 when he attended a dinner in Glasgow in honour of Daniel O'Connell, the Irish political radical and campaigner for Roman Catholic rights. He was severely criticised by his presbytery and the Synod of Glasgow and Ayr and by the local newspaper, the *Paisley Advertiser*. The outcome of this seems to be that Brewster began to enjoy courting controversy. Donald Smith has claimed that Brewster was 'the unique exception' to the 'almost unrelieved picture of Christian prophetic failure and social conformity in mid-nineteenth century Scotland'.[17] The work of Brewster's neighbour in Paisley, Robert Burns, and his contemporary in Glasgow, Robert Buchanan, raises questions about that judgement. If what Brewster said had a prophetic ring to it, the power of his words was frequently drowned out by the effect of his actions.

Brewster was a popular preacher. Even one of his fiercest critics had to admit, somewhat grudgingly:

> Mr Brewster has a crowd of followers. His preaching talent attracts the learned, his patriotism the mob. The most remarkable extremes meet within the dimly lighted old Abbey, on a Sabbath, to listen to him They are of two classes. By both, we believe, with his views of the Christian ministry, he deals honestly and conscientiously – the rich are not flattered and the poor are not scorned.[18]

His sermons, however, were not to the liking of the officers of the Paisley garrison who regularly attended worship in the Abbey and who eventually stopped church parades when Brewster was preaching. In 1842 seven of the sermons he preached were the subject of a libel (a formal indictment charging Brewster with misconduct) in the Presbytery of Paisley, and proceedings against him were only dropped in the wake of the Disruption.

Three political themes emerge from Brewster's sermons.[19] A decade before Marx and Engels produced *The Communist Manifesto*, Brewster interpreted his country's history and its economic condition in terms of a class struggle. He described the aristocracy as having taken away land that rightly belonged to the people and having used the hereditary principle to deny to all what they gave to their descendants. All wealth, he said, is the product of man's labour and those who create the wealth have a right to expect that it will be used to provide for their subsistence. The owners of industry, however, use the profits for themselves. Mechanisation, which ought to have resulted in cheaper food and clothing for those involved in production, had led to workers being forced to accept lower wages, the equivalent of the slave owner's whip. In exactly the same way, landed proprietors had taken the profits resulting from improvements in agricultural methods and passed none of their benefits on to labourers. Brewster believed there would inevitably be violent conflict between freedom and oppression unless 'the right-minded among us who sympathise with the people, will come fearlessly forward and stand on the right side'.[20]

Brewster saw the class struggle in a religious context. Whereas God had provided an abundant supply of food for all humanity, those whose work produced the food received the smallest share of it while the Corn Laws deprived many more of the

> bounty of heaven, take the bread out of the mouth of famishing industry, and transfer it back into the hands of wasteful idleness and thankless profligacy [and] the people are stripped of their rights and robbed of their property, and deprived of their liberty, and as effectually reduced to servitude and crushed under the yoke of a Master Class, as if they were actually the property of that class, and were subjected to the will of individual owners.[21]

During the Napoleonic wars, foreign imports were scarce and costly because of the danger the war posed to shipping. Domestic landowners, who dominated parliament until the Reform Act of 1832, found it profitable to turn land over to wheat, but when the end of the war seemed likely to lead to domestic grain production being subject again to foreign competition, the Corn Laws were passed, prohibiting the import of foreign corn until domestic production reached an extremely high level. Brewster's opinion of the Corn Laws is the second political theme to emerge from his sermons, in which he condemned the laws for robbing the poor of a third of their earnings, giving it to rapacious landlords.

The third area of political controversy that Brewster's sermons frequently addressed was the operation of the Poor Law. As was pointed out in the account of Robert Burns' *Dissertations*, in most areas of Scotland provision for the poor was made by means of voluntary collections and resources provided by Heritors and Kirk Sessions. Parishes in the Borders, however, frequently adopted a policy of imposing legal assessments on Heritors. Unlike Robert Burns in the earlier days of his ministry, Brewster was a strong supporter of making the assessments on Heritors and Kirk Sessions legally enforceable. He said that the legal provision for poor relief was 'the property of the poor man'[22] and did not accept the widely held view that poor relief was intended to be given only occasionally, and only to those who were physically unable to work. He maintained that it was intended to assist any who were unemployed, otherwise the law prohibiting begging would clearly be evidence that the legislature was flagrantly callous. Brewster caustically pointed out to his congregation,

> Year after year have we invited your attention to this subject. Year after year have we demanded justice to the poor, but we had not the voice of the charmer in our appeals; for we could only tell you of the claims of humanity, the rights of justice, the command of God. But you will now listen to us, when we can add to these the more powerful motives of self security, and self interest.[23]

Brewster's invocation of God was more than rhetorical. His political beliefs stemmed from three significant theological convictions. First, Brewster's demand that the Church take seriously the condition of the poor was based on a conviction that has a remarkably contemporary reference: that God is on the side of the poor. In the first of the Chartist Sermons Brewster says,

> The Son of God came, especially, to the poor. He came to preach the Gospel to the poor. He came emphatically – literally as well as figuratively, temporally as well as spiritually – to 'loose the bands of wickedness and to undo heavy burdens'. And the whole of his life on earth corresponds with this character, and the whole of his blessed Gospel tends to this effect.[24]

It is this which has led William Storrar to take the view that behind Brewster's political views there was a developed incarnational theology.[25] Certainly Brewster's theology was incarnational, but it can hardly be described as 'developed'. It would be more accurate to describe Brewster as having a strong incarnational conviction whose implications grew from the days of his early works, rather than to imply that he developed a theology of the incarnation over the years. The passage quoted above is the only one in Brewster's sermons that deals with the essence of the incarnation. In his early works he refers to the humility of Jesus but in exemplary rather than incarnational terms. His interest in the incarnation is in its consequences for the style and attitude of a Christian's life. Jesus' 'condescension' is that of a spiritual guide and teacher so that

> when Christians would imitate the humility of their great pattern, they will be bowed to the dust for their unworthiness before God ... but in their intercourse with the world they will not be required to abase themselves before the proud and the worthless.

Brewster's second fundamental conviction was that Christian faith and ministry were to be expressed politically. There are no grounds, he said, for assuming that the biblical understanding of oppression and deliverance is spiritual. The prophetic tradition in the Old Testament shows that political involvement is part of the profession of religion. Brewster shrewdly observed that when a preacher commends obedience to rulers, that is not considered to be political, but if he raises the question of rulers' obligations to their subjects, that is regarded as preaching politics. Third, Brewster viewed the Church as an institution which had as its primary function the protection of the poor and the weak against the rich and the powerful. Brewster always analysed the Church's history in terms of what he saw as its support for the poor and its aligning itself with the rich, and the extent of its promotion of freedom from oppression.

Brewster first openly associated himself with the Chartist cause in November 1838, when he addressed a local Chartist organisation, the Renfrewshire Political Union, in support of Chartism achieving its ends by moral force rather than physical violence. The next month, Brewster chaired a public meeting on Calton Hill in Edinburgh which endorsed the policy of moral force. In what is clear evidence that Brewster saw himself as the leading Chartist in Scotland, he immediately published a personal address to the Chartist movement which secretaries of local associations were to read at their next meeting. This provoked Fergus O'Connor, who hitherto had been regarded as the Chartists' leader, to come to Scotland, and the exchanges between the two were virulent, though O'Connor's language was more in keeping with his demands for physical force than was Brewster's in support of moral force. 'Listen now, my friends,' Brewster said,

> to the insolent contempt with which your enemies are assailing you. Hear the paeans they are chanting over the discomfiture and humiliation of the poor Physicals ... The folly of those who have forced themselves into the front of the Radical movement has been long apparent to the great bulk of

the people ... You must either convert the misleaders of the movement by a determined expression of opinion and an unequivocal avowal of principle, or you must get rid of them by the formation of new unions.

Brewster's actions and speeches further divided the Chartist movement and drove moderate men away from the cause of moral force. He was unable to make the compromises necessary in politics. At a time when there were suggestions that Chartists might make common cause with others who were prepared to support one or other of their aims but not all of them, Brewster issued another open address, refusing to associate with anyone else: 'I will demand the People's Charter and nothing less.'[26] By this time his influence was beginning to wane and

> his spell was broken and there was an increasing tendency to discount him as an uncompromising priest who drew £300 a year from the Church of whose principles he disapproved but was ready to sacrifice the unity of the movement for the sake of his dogmatism.[27]

The fact that Brewster was the only minister of the Church to give support to the Chartist movement gives substance to Brewster's reputation for radicalism. However, the lack of political judgement which Brewster showed, his obsessive concern with his own position and the impression he gave of dogmatic infallibility all raise the question of whether his involvement achieved much more than personal gratification. It certainly bears out the judgement of his obituarist that

> the pertinacity with which he embraced the most extreme views on public questions, and the stubbornness with which he maintained his own particular crotchets materially diminished the influence which he might have commanded, not merely in his own immediate neighbourhood but throughout the Kingdom.[28]

It was when Brewster's role in the Chartist movement began to diminish that he found expression for his aggressive concern for the underprivileged in the conditions of poverty he encountered in the narrow streets around Paisley Abbey. A public controversy in which he became involved illustrates how Brewster could lose support for a good cause by using extravagant language, personal abuse and habitual intolerance. Several times he claimed to the Abbey Kirk Session that the Heritors were not meeting their commitments to the poor. In June 1839 the Kirk Session received a petition 'from twenty four heads of families in great destitution'. Brewster blamed Walter Millar, the Superintendent of Poor Relief and an elder in the Abbey, and he said so publicly. At several Kirk Session meetings chaired by Brewster, Millar was criticised, and then on Christmas Day Brewster wrote to the

Paisley Advertiser boasting that Millar had been found guilty of gross neglect. When the matter was referred to the Presbytery of Paisley, however, Brewster's treatment of Millar was severely criticised. The Presbytery expressed regret at the language Brewster used about an elder and concluded that Millar's responsibilities were not to the Kirk Session but to the Kirk Session and Heritors jointly and that there was no evidence to justify forcing Millar to resign. The Presbytery instructed that the Kirk Session minutes dealing with the dispute with Millar be erased by the Presbytery Clerk. A letter Brewster sent Millar, and which he subsequently published, was typical of Brewster's dealings with people with whom he disagreed:

> Nerve yourself once more, Mr Walter. You have given me an opportunity of rebutting a very malignant statement which the parish harpies have for some time been very busy in propagating, namely that in taking the part of the poor I have been influenced solely by a desire to punish the Heritors for not granting me an augmentation of stipend ... Every one connected with the business of the parish knows well, that for upwards of twenty years I have advocated the claims of the poor; demanding larger aliments for paupers, and exemption from assessment for the labouring classes; and in order to obtain my object, making a voluntary offer to pay the proportion of my own income, though exempted by law; which offer, however, was refused by the meeting under the absurd pretence that they would be obliged to assess other ministers.[29]

Similar letters about others, published in various newspapers, abound.

It would be wrong to deny that Patrick Brewster has an important place in the history of the Church of Scotland and its social development. As Stewart Mechie wrote,

> one may hail him as a modern representative of a tradition ... which asserted the right of the Christian minister to comment on public affairs and apply the law of God as he learned it from Scripture to the laws of the land and custom in every sphere of the national life.[30]

It is to Brewster's credit that he was a powerful opponent of slavery and a strong supporter of Catholic emancipation, though he did not grant to a Roman Catholic the freedom to marry his daughter. His passionate concern for the poor is clear. What is not so clear, however, is whether he deserves the exclusive significance he has been given. His preaching, though powerful and popular, was not enhanced by the extreme language he often used or the personalised attacks in which he indulged. His social theology was expressed in slogans rather than being thoughtfully developed, and his effect on the administration of support for the poor was adversely affected by the controversies which he seemed to relish. His contribution to Chartism was not great and, largely due to his arrogance, was short-lived. His career, however, illustrates how even someone as committed to social reform as Brewster was could not see any alternative to support for the poor being administered through and within a territorial and parochial system.

VERY REVD DR NORMAN MACLEOD

When Norman Macleod died at the age of sixty in 1872, Dean Stanley wrote of him in *The Times* that he 'represented Scottish Protestantism more than any other single man. Under and around him men would gather who would gather round no-one else. When he spoke it was felt to be the voice, the best voice of Scotland.'[31] He founded the popular magazine *Good Words*, which he edited from 1860 until his death in 1872. By 1870 its circulation had risen from 25,000 on the sale of the first issue to 80,000. He was a most effective parish minister, organising his congregation to provide facilities for the disadvantaged, dividing his parish into districts, ensuring that each district was well visited and supported, and providing adult education classes, a reading room, recreational facilities and cheap food for some of the poorest people in Glasgow. Macleod persuaded his congregation to join him in visits to the poorest parts of the parish. He established sewing and evening classes to increase the chances of employment and formed a loan fund to provide funds for those who wanted better housing or personal improvement. Evening services were held for those who could not afford to pay seat rents or felt out of place among the well-to-do who worshipped in the morning, and over a thousand attended them regularly. He was also a superb writer and storyteller who used *Good Words* as a vehicle for the sort of liberal approach to social issues that he adopted and the social concern that he expressed. While Norman Macleod's social conscience and concern is unquestionable, suggestions that he departed markedly from the prevailing social theology require to be treated cautiously. A. C. Cheyne, and later Peter Hillis in his detailed study of the composition of the Barony Kirk Session and congregation, quote Macleod, writing the year he was inducted to the Barony:

> The common idea at present is that the whole function of the Church is to preach and teach the gospel; while it is left to other organisations, infidel ones they may be, to meet all the other varied wants of our suffering people. And what is this but virtually to say to them, the Church of Christ has nothing to do as a society with your bodies, only with your souls, and that too, but in the way of teaching. Let infidels, then, give you better housing or better clothing, and seek to gratify your tastes and improve your social state; with all this, and a thousand other things needful for you as men, we have nothing to do. What is this, too, but to give these men the impression that

Christ gives them truth merely on Sabbath through ministers, but that He has nothing to do with what is given them every day of the week through other channels.[32]

It is doubtful whether this is as clear a departure from the prevailing social theology as Hillis makes it out to be. Norman Macleod is certainly articulating the need for the Church to be concerned with social conditions, but that concern was already part of the prevailing social theology, which held that the most effective way to improve social conditions was through the Church's missionary, evangelistic and educational work. That is precisely why Macleod followed the pattern of territorial ministry set by Thomas Chalmers, and Norman Macleod, like Robert Buchanan, accepted without question that people's social conditions would be improved if they connected themselves to the Church and its worship. He wrote:

> If ever society is to be regenerated, it is by the agency of living brothers and sisters in the Lord; and every plan, however apparently wise, for recovering mankind from their degradation, and which does not make use of the personal ministrations of Christian men and women as an essential part of it, its very life is doomed, we think, to perish.[33]

It is clear from a very significant but neglected sermon, published shortly after his death, that Macleod envisaged no fundamental change in the structured order of society. He asked what results there would be if God's will were to be established on earth:

> Society would remain, with relationships continuing as they were, but purged of envy and jealousy. Commerce would remain, but without any deception. The arts would remain, but only to beautify human existence. Amusement and leisure would remain, but devoid of dissipating temptation. Sickness and suffering would remain but they would be accepted as the opportunity to display meekness and faith. And rich and poor would remain: but who can measure to what extent their relative position would be affected by the love and righteousness now possessed by both – by prudence, industry and sobriety, on the one hand; and by considerate kindness and liberality and sympathy on the other? If alms were needed, the poor would become richer in the love that supplied them; and the rich would also be made richer, by giving with the knowledge that it was more blessed to give than to receive.[34]

Macleod wrote an article for *Good Words* in which he told the fictional story of a man sitting on a stone by the roadside in old fustian clothes 'on the coldest of cold days'. He said he had been looking for work for three weeks. The passing Samaritan took the man to his home, where he found there was no food in the house for him, his wife and his five children, no fire and hardly any bedclothes. Shortly afterwards the man attempted to hang himself but was cut down by his wife in time to save his life. He said, 'As an able bodied man I could get nae relief from the parish; but I kent if I were deid, they wid be obliged tae help my widow and orphans.' Macleod commented that thanks to help from the passing Samaritan, two pounds 'restored him to comparative comfort; a note to an employer obtained him work, and he has never wanted since'.[35] Macleod used that story to introduce three of his firm convictions with regard to parochial, palliative social work: a little money can make a big difference; personal contact and visitation are vitally important; and 'while legal charity spends its hundred of pounds, Christian charity, if its dispensers are properly organised, would with its tens attain, in every respect, higher results'.[36]

Good Words was not universally approved of as a suitable publication for young people. A group of anonymous journalists attacked Macleod's editorship in a series of pamphlets on the grounds that contributors such as Charles Kingsley and Dean Stanley were supporters of a Broad Church, rather than the Evangelical Alliance to which, they said, Macleod had once belonged. They criticised contributors, and especially the editor himself, because they believed they interpreted the atonement in terms of love rather than satisfaction, at best minimised and at worst ignored original sin, and encouraged a lax attitude towards Sunday observance.[37]

Norman Macleod's social vision still harked back to the rural vision, both of which by his time in the Barony were no longer remotely relevant. Nor did his social vision foresee the transformation of society. The theologian Robert Flint, who was close to him in the years when he was an assistant in the Barony, describes him as being 'fully alive to the importance of Churches keeping aloof, as far as possible, from the struggles in the arena of politics'. In the same article, Flint describes Macleod as 'the greatest pastor which any Scottish parish had possessed since Chalmers left St John's, Glasgow'.[38] This explains in part why Macleod did not develop his social concern into a coherent social theology; his concern was for the pastoral care of those entrusted to him and his congregation. Inevitably the extent of the social problems in the Barony parish, then comprising 87,000 souls, made him turn instinctively to the palliative measures that were so obviously and urgently needed, rather than to a rigorous critique of structural poverty which he was intellectually and temperamentally unsuited to provide. Flint wrote that Macleod 'was not in distinctive sense a theologian'. He lacked creative originality, but 'although not a great theologian, [he] exerted a great, and I believe most beneficial influence on our theology'.[39]

Burns, Buchanan and Macleod, no less than Patrick Brewster, also cast doubts on the judgement, frequently made after the publication of Donald

Smith's harsh critique, that the Church in Scotland in the middle years of the nineteenth century showed no interest in the social conditions of the poor or in tackling the problems presented by the rapidly increasing urban population. All four, however, saw the Church as the primary if not the sole agent of social reform. Patrick Brewster believed that the Church had a God-given role throughout history to support the weak and powerless, and in his own day to promote social justice. Robert Burns' *Dissertations* is a strong defence of support for the poor through the Kirk Session, and although later Burns saw the need for legal assessments, he always envisaged the Kirk Session's role in administering the proceeds continuing. Robert Buchanan was convinced that it was through evangelism and Church extension that movements for social reform would be inspired, and Norman Macleod energised and restructured the congregational life of the Barony precisely because he believed it was only through the ministrations of Christian people that poverty would be alleviated. If they were to develop a social theology that was capable of contributing to the urban crisis, the Presbyterian churches had to find a different model which would enable them to become engaged with the social issues of the late nineteenth century. It was provided for them by the young minister of Aberdeen's East Church, Robert Flint.

NOTES

1. Hurd, Douglas (2007) *Robert Peel: A Biography* (London: Phoenix), p. 263.
2. *Distress at Paisley*, The National Archive, Home Office Papers, HO/45/345.
3. Ibid.
4. Burns, Robert (1819) *Historical Dissertations on the Law and Practice of Great Britain and particularly Scotland with regard to the Poor* (Edinburgh: Peter Hill).
5. Burns, Robert F. (1871) *The Life and Times of the Rev. Robert Burns, DD* (Toronto: J. Campbell) pp. 91–2.
6. Ibid. p. 88.
7. Burns, Robert (1841) *A Plea for the Poor of Scotland, Two Lectures* (Paisley: Alexander Gardner); (1842) *Christian Patriotism in Times of Distress* (Paisley: Alexander Gardner).
8. Engels, Friedrich (1936) *Conditions of the Working Class in England* (London: Allen and Unwin), p. 38.
9. Walker, Norman L. (1877) *Robert Buchanan, An Ecclesiastical Biography* (London: Thomas Nelson).
10. Smith, *Passive Obedience and Prophetic Protest*, p. 93.

11. Buchanan, Robert (1850) *The Schoolmaster in the Wynds* (Glasgow: Blackie & Son), p. 7.
12. Buchanan, Robert (1851) *The Spiritual Destitution of the Masses in Glasgow* (Glasgow: Blackie & Son).
13. Buchanan, Robert (1851) *A Second Appeal on the Spiritual Destitution of the Masses in Glasgow* (Glasgow: Blackie & Son).
14. *Proceedings and Debates of the General Assembly of the United Free Church of Scotland* (Edinburgh: Lorimer and Chalmers, 1851), p. 304ff.
15. Brown, Callum G. (1996) 'To be aglow with civic ardours: the "Godly Commonwealth" in Glasgow 1843–1914', *Records of the Scottish Church History Society*, vol. XXVI, pp. 169–95.
16. Buchanan, *Schoolmaster in the Wynds*, p. 29.
17. Smith, *Passive Obedience and Prophetic Protest*, p. 175.
18. Smith, John (1849) *Our Scottish Clergy* (Edinburgh: Oliver and Boyd).
19. Brewster, Patrick (1842) *The Seven Chartist and Military Discourses ordered by the General Assembly to be libelled by the Presbytery of Paisley.* Quotations are from J. T. Johnston, *The Rev. Patrick Brewster: His Chartist Socialist Sermons* (Glasgow: Forward) (n.d.).
20. Ibid. p. 56.
21. Ibid. p. 31.
22. Ibid. p. 78.
23. Ibid. p. 34.
24. Ibid. p. 5.
25. Storrar, William (1990) *Scottish Identity* (Edinburgh: The Handsel Press), p. 108.
26. Quotations are from press cuttings in Brewster's uncatalogued Scrapbook, preserved in Paisley Abbey. The pages are not numbered.
27. Wilson, A. (1970) *The Chartist Movement in Scotland* (Manchester: Manchester University Press), p. 63.
28. *Glasgow Herald*, 28 March 1859.
29. Brewster, Patrick (1843) *The Legal Rights of the Poor of Scotland Vindicated* (Paisley: published by the author), p. 18.
30. Mechie, Stewart (1960) *The Church and Scottish Social Development* (London: Oxford University Press), p. 118.
31. Ferguson, Ronald (1990) *George Macleod* (London: Collins), pp. 15–16.
32. Cheyne, A. C. (1993) *The Transforming of the Kirk* (Edinburgh: Saint Andrew Press), pp. 7–8; Hillis, Peter (2007) *The Barony of Glasgow* (Edinburgh: Dunedin Academic Press), pp. 66–7.
33. Macleod, Norman (1862) *Parish Papers* (London: Alexander Strahan), p. 239.
34. Macleod, Norman (1872) 'God's will be done', *Good Words*, pp. 622–7.
35. Macleod, Norman (1866) 'How can we best relieve our deserving poor', *Good Words*, pp. 554–62.
36. Ibid. p. 142.

37. Anon. (1863) *Good Words: The Theology of its Editor and Some of its Contributors* (London: The Record Office).
38. Flint, Robert (1883) 'Norman Macleod', in *Scottish Divines, St Giles' Lectures* (Edinburgh: McNiven and Wallace), p. 439.
39. Ibid. p. 452.

2

From Church to Kingdom
Robert Flint's New Model for the Church's Engagement with Society

The Church is not the Kingdom of God, and these elements of social life, in separating themselves from the Church, have not separated themselves from the Kingdom of God

Robert Flint, sermon, 1859

In 1859, Charles Darwin published *The Origin of Species*, and in the same year, at the age of twenty-five, Robert Flint became minister of the East Church in Aberdeen. He was a very reserved and serious young man, unsure of himself on social occasions, preferring the company of his parents and sister who stayed with him in his various homes. Flint took immense care in the preparation of his sermons, revising them almost until it was time to enter the pulpit. In his first winter as a parish minister he preached a series of sermons on the parables about the Kingdom of God recorded in Matthew's Gospel Chapter 13. He repeated them two years later when he became minister of Kilconquhar in the East Neuk of Fife, and they were published in 1865, when he became Professor of Moral Philosophy at the University of St Andrews. In 1876 he was appointed to the Chair of Divinity in Edinburgh which he occupied until he retired in 1903.

Robert Flint was born in 1834 in Dumfriesshire, the son of a tenant sheep farmer. When he was ten, the family moved to Glasgow, where his father set up in business and became a member of Lauriston Free Church, which Robert attended until he was twenty years of age. His mother, however, remained within the Church of Scotland. His father always worshipped in the Free Church, even though he stayed with Robert in his various homes. At the age of fourteen, Robert began ten years of study at the University of Glasgow. He was a contemporary of Norman Macleod's brother Donald, who wrote of Flint:

I came to know him well as he was intimate with several of my student friends who used to gather in the picturesque court of the old university in the High Street. As I recollect him at the time he was pale and bore the imprint of severe study. He was somewhat shy and stood rather aloof from the rowdy political groups which fought the Rectorial Elections. His intellectual power was even then recognised, and we all anticipated for him a distinguished future.

Dr Robert Howie, who was to have a distinguished ministry first in the Wynds of Glasgow and then in Govan, and who became Moderator of the Free Church's General Assembly, was another contemporary at Glasgow University:

> My chief recollection of Flint in his student days was seeing him carry off great bundles of prizes in different classes and especially those in theology, and prizes for work done during summer vacation, for he was a keen, able and very successful student, and took little interest in any of the sports or political organisations connected with the University.[1]

Considering that Flint worshipped in the Free Church, Robert Howie must have expected that he would join him as a student for its ministry. Flint believed that he would find more theological freedom in the Church of Scotland than in the Free Church so he joined the congregation of St George's Church in Buchanan Street in 1855, paying for one seat at ten shillings per annum. During Flint's final year as a Glasgow student, in 1857, he was appointed the missionary of the recently formed Glasgow Elders' Association. The area where he was sent to work was around the foot of the High Street, in between the parishes of Norman Macleod and Robert Buchanan. He made an average of 100 visits each week and was paid £50 a year. The following year he became first missionary and then assistant to Norman Macleod in the Barony, succeeding Norman's brother Donald, who had just been inducted to his first charge in Lauder. Flint's work was mainly in the Barony's mission stations in Kelvinhaugh and Port Dundas.

When the politician and social reformer Lord Shaftesbury visited the city to which the Flint family was about to move, he wrote in his diary:

> Walked through the 'dreadful' parts of this amazing city; it is a small square plot intersected by small alleys, like gutters, crammed with houses, dunghills and human beings; hence arise nine tenths of the disease and nine tenths of the crime in Glasgow; and well it may. Health would be impossible in such a climate; the air tainted by exhalation from the most stinking and stagnant sources, a pavement never dry, in lanes not broad enough to admit a wheelbarrow. And is moral propriety and moral cleanliness, so to speak, more probable? Quite the reverse.[2]

Shaftesbury asks rhetorically about moral propriety and cleanliness because there was a widespread view at the time that the squalor of Glasgow's East

End, and the slums of other cities too, were caused by a lack of morality. If those who lived in the conditions Shaftesbury described could be brought under the influence of the Church they would develop the moral character that would drive them either to improve the conditions in which they lived or else escape from them. What became known by the clumsy phrase 'non-church going' was regarded as a primary cause of destitution. It is mistaken to assume that because the Church focused on conversion and believed that would lead to social improvement, it was institutionally callous or wilfully or prophetically silent on the extent of urban poverty, as Robert Burns, Robert Buchanan and Norman Macleod as well as Patrick Brewster demonstrated.

THE KINGDOM OF CHRIST UPON EARTH: THE CONTEXT

Somehow the Church had to escape from the trap of regarding the evangelical effectiveness of the parish church and minister as essential to the reduction of poverty and the improvement of social conditions. Robert Flint's book *Christ's Kingdom upon Earth*, which contained his sermons on the parables of the Kingdom, gave the Church a new model to describe its relationship with society. He argued for cooperation with secular agencies and insisted that this would not undermine the influence of the Church. Put simply, cooperation was necessary practically but, more important, required theologically.

A great deal of Flint's understanding of the Kingdom of God is to be found in the works of mainly European scholars in the preceding century and a half, although Flint cannot be said to have followed the views of any of them in anything approaching their entirety. He saw the sweep of history as a gradual progression towards the Kingdom of God, through the overcoming of evil. Where evil exists, he said, God's Kingdom has not been realised. In being totally convinced of the march of human progress, Flint was typical of his day, which has been described as one in which progress became almost an article of faith, its denial an act of blasphemy. Although Immanuel Kant (1724–1804) was a philosopher rather than a theologian, the Kingdom of God was crucial to his view of religion. He regarded the Kingdom as instituted for the purpose of avoiding what is evil and cultivating what is good in humanity. When Flint writes that where evil exists the Kingdom of God has not yet been realised, there is an echo of Kant's 'ethical commonwealth', though Flint would not have accepted Kant's reduction of the Kingdom to matters of morality and conscience, and he envisages the contrast between good and evil much more as a struggle between God and Satan, taking place throughout biblical and subsequent history and in contemporary society.

New Testament scholars later became very interested in what Jesus meant when he talked about the Kingdom of God. In 1835 a Tübingen scholar, David Friedrich Strauss (1808–74) published a *Life of Christ*. Strauss' view was that Jesus envisaged a messianic kingdom in which he would restore the throne of Israel following the intervention of legions of angels sent by the heavenly Father. The Frenchman Ernest Renan in 1863 also published a *Life of Christ*. In Renan's lyrical, fanciful picture of Jesus and the Palestine of his day Jesus was forced, towards the end of his life, to envisage the Kingdom coming as a sudden and apocalyptic eruption into the world. But Renan says this was

> a transient error ... the Jesus who founded the Kingdom of God, the Kingdom of the meek and the humble was the Jesus of early life, of these pure and chaste days when the voice of the Father re-echoed within him in clearer times. It was then, for some months, perhaps a year, that God truly dwelt on earth.[3]

A churchman whom Flint greatly admired, John Cairns, later Principal of the United Presbyterian Church's theological hall, preached a sermon for the National Bible Society which was an attack on the theories of Strauss and Renan.[4] In his sermons on the Kingdom in *Christ's Kingdom upon Earth*, Flint praises Cairns' criticisms of Strauss and Renan and describes Renan's book as 'superficial and saddening'. He says that Renan regarded Jesus' teaching about the Kingdom as 'vague, various and conflicting'. Sometimes it was the reign of the poor and the outcast, with Jesus a kind of democratic head; at other times it was the literal accomplishment of the apocalyptic vision of Daniel and Enoch; and at other times and often a spiritual Kingdom that rules the individual soul.[5]

Flint expresses very little interest in when Jesus expected the Kingdom would come, because he is certain that the Kingdom of God began with the life, death and resurrection of Jesus of Nazareth, in the same way as a mustard seed contains within itself the germ of the whole of its subsequent development. Flint is less concerned with Jesus' self-consciousness than he is with the development throughout history of the Kingdom of God from 'the little seed corn which had to be dropped into the ground and die ere the earth could bear a harvest of righteousness and peace'.[6] Flint's view is that God's Kingdom arrived with what later scholars were to call 'the Jesus event', and so it is not a pattern, structure or blueprint that can be applied and still less can it be imposed. It is an ideal that emerged in Jesus and grew as human unreliability was replaced by divine law, human wickedness by divine holiness. Albrecht Ritschl (1822–89) also believed that the Kingdom developed gradually, but there the similarity with Flint ends. Following Kant, Ritschl said that the Kingdom is the result and product of common human ethical activity. He believed that the Kingdom of God is made up of those who believe in Christ, inasmuch as they treat one another with love, without regard to differences of sex, rank or race, and so bring about the moral fellowship that is the Kingdom. Flint regarded the Kingdom as God's reign in people's lives, inspiring them to act in a way that made society more equal, more just and more religious and therefore closer to the ideal of God's Kingdom on earth. When the Gospel produces a change within the individual human heart, society will be changed by transformed individuals. Ritschl regarded the Kingdom as more akin to a 'realm' than a 'reign', a defined group of people with a common moral purpose. Although Flint had little respect for Ritschlian theology generally, he agreed with Ritschl in one important regard. He shared Ritschl's view that the Church could never be wholly identified with the Kingdom of God, but was rather a means to an end, though Flint would never have accepted Ritschl's description of the Church as the ethical unification of the human race through activity inspired by the motive of love. Flint regarded the Church as a society that owed its origin not merely to the will of its members but to the will of Christ. The view that it is simply a human voluntary association of Christians is one Flint regarded as profoundly inadequate.

The English scholar and Christian socialist F. D. Maurice (1805–72) published his two-volume study *The Kingdom of Christ* in 1838. In many ways Robert Flint's sermons on the Kingdom of God are a direct response to Maurice's conviction that the Kingdom that Christ came to establish was identical to the Church, and that the signs of the Kingdom were the ordinances of religion. Maurice had written,

> If you ask us 'Where are the signs of the Kingdom? What are the proofs of its establishment on earth?' We answer boldly, 'every Church that you see around you – every baptism to which you bring your children – every sacrament by which you bind yourself, and by which you see others bind themselves to the Head and Lord of the whole body, is a witness to its establishment'.[7]

Flint would have agreed with Maurice that Christianity cannot be separated from the world of politics, but he would have disagreed with his contention that there are two principles, 'one Christian, one secular, and that the two can never be brought into agreement together; therefore let Christianity claim dominion over all the ordinary, civil affairs of men, and deny the right of the secular principle over any of them'.[8]

THE KINGDOM OF CHRIST UPON EARTH: THE CONTENT

Several themes run through Flint's sermons on the Kingdom. First, he saw the emergence of God's Kingdom against the background and within the context of a continuing struggle between God and Satan, good and evil. Where evil exists, God's Kingdom has not yet been realised. Second, and as a corollary to the struggle between good and evil, Flint believed that God brings order out of the conflict of innumerable human wills. The Kingdom has been advancing, despite opposition, since Christ's departure from earth. Flint recognised, therefore, that the Kingdom of God is an ideal that emerges, develops and grows, and so the nature parables are the most appropriate way to describe its effect on society. The Kingdom emerged from the germ of Christ's life and death, and it advances as subsequent human labour and effort are added to it. In his sermon on the parable of the sower, Flint argued that because the Kingdom grows and develops, it is not possible to envisage a return to some primitive simplicity. Thus force and persecution are never justified in the cause of the Kingdom of God, and any attempt to make sectarian or denominational principles a condition of Church privileges or Church membership is sinful.

Flint pointed out that the growth of a plant is, nevertheless, an inadequate symbol for the Kingdom of God because the Gospel, unlike an individual plant, must relate to and have an effect on the community where it is proclaimed. So the parable of the leaven, which spreads through the dough and alters its nature and properties, is a more appropriate way to describe the effect of the Kingdom of God on society. The Kingdom pervades society, and even where the Gospel is not accepted, it nevertheless so infiltrates the structures of society that it changes them:

> The Gospel is not without influence even where it is not closed with as the power of God unto salvation. It so far imbues, or at least modifies, by its spirit all the laws, institutions and usages of society, that none, not even those most hostile to it, live as they would have done if it had not been. It improves both the characters and conduct of men in every case, although it may be only seldom that it works a genuine conversion in them.[9]

It is against that background that Flint made his most specific comments with regard to the Kingdom of God and the Church. He used the strongest of language to reject any identification of the Kingdom of God with the Church, which he described as 'the most common and not the least pernicious' of the erroneous views of the Kingdom of God. Since the arts, literature and science, and indeed the state itself, have separated themselves from the Church, they have been able independently to contribute towards the Kingdom of God.[10]

> Are we to conclude that all these things have become atheistical, irreligious, unchristian, because they have separated themselves from the Church, asserted rights of their own, and jealously guard these rights? Assuredly no.

The Church is not the Kingdom of God, and these elements of social life, in separating themselves from the Church, have not separated themselves from the Kingdom of God; nay, by the very act of rejecting the control of the Church they set aside the mediation of the Church between them and the Kingdom of God, and secured for themselves, as a portion of their independence, the right of standing in immediate contact with the Word and the Kingdom of God. Before their independence they were related to the Kingdom of God only through their connection with the Church; now, since their independence, they may justly claim to be portions of the Kingdom of God, each one of them as much a portion of it as the Church itself.[11]

That is a crucial passage for the development of social theology in the nineteenth-century Scottish Church. By the 1890s, when the Presbyterian Churches were ready to accept that they had a role in social development and were beginning to develop a social theology, the conviction that the Church and the Kingdom of God were separate was virtually regarded as axiomatic. There was disagreement over whether, or to what extent, the Church should advance the Kingdom of God by being socially and politically engaged, but there was almost complete agreement that the Church and the Kingdom of God were not one and the same. It was also widely accepted that, as Flint went on to conclude from the separation of the Church and the Kingdom, agencies other than the Church could contribute towards the realisation of the Kingdom, and, as we shall see, that too was important and influential in the development of the Church's social theology. There are those, Flint pointed out, who may bemoan that the power of the Church is reduced by 'elements in social life' separating themselves from the Church; but what is lost to the Church is not lost to the Kingdom of God. If the Church had recognised that it was only the means to an end then less time would have been spent on controversies, and the Church would have avoided being used as an instrument of state persecution on religious grounds. The Church can accommodate itself to other agencies in society, knowing what is its own, inviolable sphere. As well as enabling the Church to include other elements in society in the advancement of the Kingdom of God, Flint's encouragement of the Church to have sufficient confidence in itself and its own 'inviolable sphere' allowed the Church to escape from the view that restricted Brewster and Burns, Buchanan and Macleod: that the Church itself, and its evangelical imperative, were essential to social progress.

Another dominant theme in Flint's understanding of the Kingdom of God is that the Kingdom becomes a power in society when and because someone becomes personally committed to it. It 'begins within', by replacing an individual's unpredictable conduct and wickedness with surrender to God's will and holiness. When the Gospel works on the heart of a person then it persuades that person to work to change society, and if the Gospel does not produce that determination to change society, then it has not been fully effective. Individuals who have understood the Gospel are committed to hasten in the Kingdom of God where they are.

The significance of Flint's views on the Kingdom of God, however, does not lie in his view of the effect on society of a committed Christian person. In that, he is saying nothing more or less than Norman Macleod or Robert Buchanan did. *Christ's Kingdom upon Earth* has been largely ignored but it was hugely influential in arguing that as a consequence of the separation of Church and Kingdom, through forms of public service outside the work of the Church and the commitment to social justice of those who might not have a personal faith, the Kingdom of God nevertheless advances.

> The Kingdom of God is not to be established among us in this country solely by the services of the sanctuary, or directly religious exercises and instruction. A legislator by obtaining good laws, a poet by writing ennobling verses, a country gentleman by an active interest in the wellbeing of those who are on his estates and in his neighbourhood, and every class of men by the faithful discharge of their duties in commerce or trade, science or art, may help and hasten on the coming of the Kingdom of God without entering into the ecclesiastical sphere of action.[12]

Flint's views on the Kingdom of God were crucial in providing the theological context in which ministers in Glasgow felt able to outline a religious critique of the conditions of deprivation that prevailed in the city and to endorse, from a religious perspective, the work of the secular agencies that attempted to improve these conditions. What Flint's work on the Kingdom of God did was to provide the critical apparatus that men like Norman Macleod and Robert Buchanan had lacked in their examination of the Church's role in the developing social crisis in the west of Scotland. Although Flint was a very young man when he preached and published his sermons on the Kingdom, he continued to advocate the views expressed in his first book in his university lectures, his sermons, his later published work and his contribution to various conferences and congresses held by the Church of Scotland at which he was an invited speaker.

THE EDINBURGH PROFESSOR

In the lectures he gave to students for the ministry in the University of Edinburgh Flint always included an exposition of the parables of the Kingdom,[13] and he relied very heavily on material from his book of sermons. Where there are changes from *Christ's Kingdom upon Earth* in his Edinburgh University lectures they always have the effect of sharpening the clear distinction he drew between the Church and the Kingdom of God. He introduced students to the Kingdom of God in a different way from the introduction to it in his sermons, starting by spelling out the consequences for the Church of a belief that the Church and the Kingdom are not identical. The Church

> may not lay its commands upon other institutions, as if it belonged to the Kingdom of God and they not, but has to teach them that, by right if not in fact, they belong to the Kingdom of God, as much as itself – thus awakening them – art, literature, science, commerce, Government – to a sense of their true dignity, of their high vocation.

He clearly wanted those who would be preachers and leaders in the local church to realise the context in which their ministry would be exercised.

The one place in his lectures where Flint modified an important view he expressed in his published sermons was in his treatment of the parable of the sower, in which he appeared to be responding to the charge that his refusal to identify the Church with the Kingdom meant that the contribution of those in the secular world, whom he harnessed in the Kingdom's service, was on an equal footing with that of those who were inspired by the Gospel. In his sermon he explained that the different types of soil described in the parable referred to different categories of people who responded, which allowed him to include those who contributed to the Kingdom through public service. He omitted this passage in his lectures and instead talked about the different types of soil reflecting different forms of receptiveness to the Gospel, which of course leads to those who have heard and understood having the greatest impact. He said to his students what he did not say to his congregations, that even if worldly people appear to be as valuable as people of faith, the difference in motivation, which lies in the imperative of the Gospel, is crucial.

In two collections of sermons, addresses and published articles, Flint continued to repeat his views on the Kingdom of God. The most significant pulpit reference to the Kingdom of God is in a sermon he preached in St Giles' Cathedral during the General Assembly of 1881. One of Flint's constant themes was that Jesus spoke so little about the Church and so frequently of the Kingdom that the doctrine of the Church must emerge from the doctrine of the Kingdom. When Flint was invited to preach before the General Assembly this theme occupied an important part of the sermon. He told the commissioners to the Assembly,

> The Church exists solely for the sake of the Kingdom; it accomplishes its end only in the measure in which it extends and builds up the Kingdom of God on earth. To identify it with the Kingdom is to confound the means with the end – to disregard the very letter of Christ's teaching – to contradict its whole spirit and character – and to deny His real claims to kingship.[14]

In another sermon preached in St Giles' on the occasion of the meeting of the first General Council of the Presbyterian Alliance in 1877, Flint said that social questions are more important than ecclesiastical ones, and that Church unity was something which ought not to be 'striven for' but should emerge through the principle of growth, thus reflecting the governing principle at the heart of the Kingdom of God.[15] He used a sermon to the National Association for the Advancement of Art to repeat a favourite theme, that the contribution of art and the artist has considerable social significance, and as such it advances the Kingdom of God.[16]

One of the papers that Flint included in his collection of academic studies was on 'Christ's teaching as to the Kingdom of God'.[17] In it he attempts, in more detail than elsewhere, to analyse the concept of the Kingdom of God from a biblical perspective. He points out that Jesus did not provide a formal definition of the Kingdom, but rather drew attention to the characteristics of the Kingdom, which Flint says are the surrender of an individual to the will of God, repentance and faith. Jesus' teaching about the Kingdom was original in three respects: the Kingdom was connected to Jesus' own messianic consciousness; he revealed God as Father; and his miracles showed the nature of the Kingdom. This paper is, for someone of Flint's theological originality, remarkably cautious and conservative in its approach to biblical scholarship. He was, of course, suspicious of 'higher criticism' and advised divinity students that 'it is not the work of the Christian minister to discuss in the pulpit, and before people who cannot possibly judge of them with adequate knowledge, the hypotheses debated in the schools of biblical criticism'. Even so it is remarkable that over twenty years after the Free Church scholar Robertson Smith questioned whether Jesus' attributing the authorship of the Pentateuch to Moses was sufficient grounds for accepting it, and when in the Free Church George Adam Smith was repeating Robertson's views and easily avoided the fate of Robertson Smith, Flint had no hesitation in accepting the Mosaic authorship of the Pentateuch. His somewhat pedestrian references to Mark's theme of the messianic secret take no account of Wrede and his work, with which Flint would have been familiar.

In 1899, Flint spoke at the first of three official Congresses that the Church of Scotland held between then and 1904.[18] His subject was the attitude of the Church to social and economic movements, and he described the Kingdom of God as the underlying and unifying idea in both Old and New Testaments. Were the Church more sympathetic to the social problem, 'the Kingdom of God would assuredly make a wonderful advance'. Specifically, Flint said that poverty is an evil, and, 'as it is always largely remediable, society should do its best to remove it'. Neither money itself, nor wages, will solve the social problem because economic conditions depend on getting the prior intellectual, moral and social conditions right. Flint appealed for the Church to support other bodies that aim at tackling destitution, alleviating suffering and healing disease. Specifically he asked that congregations might devote some of their offerings to these bodies. He gave his endorsement to movements such as savings banks, life insurance companies, friendly societies, cooperatives in industry and trades unionism, which, 'despite errors and evils it may have been responsible for is a necessity'.

Several of Flint's Scottish academic contemporaries felt it necessary to respond to his view of the Kingdom of God. His most severe critic was James Cooper (1846–1922), a successor of Flint's in the East Church of St Nicholas in Aberdeen and later Professor of Ecclesiastical History at the University of Glasgow, who was someone for whom Flint had a high regard both personally and professionally. He was one of the group for whom Flint's successor in Edinburgh, W. P. Paterson, coined the name 'Scoto-Catholics'. Cooper told the congregation of the East Church that the Church is 'the Kingdom which [Christ] founded for diffusing the faith and building up his people'.[19] He said to a Church of England audience that the Kingdom of God was the body of Christ.[20] And in his inaugural lecture at Glasgow University he described the Church as the Kingdom of heaven on earth.[21]

In 1884, James Candlish, Professor of Systematic Theology at the Free Church College in Glasgow, chose the Kingdom of God as the subject for his Cunningham Lectures. Candlish pointed out that it had often been assumed that the terms Church and Kingdom were synonymous but that 'recently' it had been held doctrinally to maintain the separation of the two. Candlish was only prepared to recognise a distinction between the two, not the separation that Flint regarded as fundamental. He said that the Church and the Kingdom of God had to be distinguished from each other, not because they were separate but because the terms were used to distinguish two distinct aspects of discipleship. The Church describes the disciples of Christ as a religious society, the Kingdom of God as a moral society. The special functions of the Church are the exercises of worship, and have to do with the relation of men to God; those of the Kingdom of God are the fulfilment of the law of love and the doing of the will of God in all departments and relations of human life.[22]

Five years after Candlish published his view on the Kingdom of God, his colleague in Glasgow's Trinity College, Alexander Balmain Bruce, gave the subject a very different treatment, which brought him into conflict with the Free Church because in it he repeated a view he had already expressed in an earlier work on the miracles: that the Gospels were not free from error.[23] Flint would not have shared Bruce's admiration for German biblical criticism, which regarded some passages in the Gospels as owing more to the reflection of the Christian community that produced them than to statements of the historical Jesus or activities attributed to him. Bruce, however, followed Flint both in his method of examining the Kingdom of God and in his conclusions about it. Like Flint, his description of the Kingdom of God was derived from the parables in which Jesus described it, and his interpretation of the parables was in many places very similar to Flint's. He was also as determined as Flint to separate Church and Kingdom.

Like Flint, Bruce believed that the Kingdom advances on earth but its ultimate realisation lies beyond earth, that the Kingdom is greater than the Church, even the Church at its highest and best, and that the Kingdom of God includes many outside the community of faith. He said that he was disposed to think that to a large and increasing extent, the moral worth of society is to be found outside the Church, 'separated from it not by godlessness but by exceptional moral earnestness'. Bruce believed that the Kingdom of God included those who had unconsciously expressed a love for Christ in their concern for the poor and the suffering. If the visible Church failed to live up to its calling, then it would disappear, 'leaving the spirit of Christ free room to make a new experiment, under happier auspices, at self-realisation'.[24]

On the Continent, studies of Jesus' understanding of the Kingdom of God moved far from the view Flint had taken of it. Johannes Weiss (1863–1914) concluded that Jesus expected the Kingdom to come through the miraculous intervention of God so soon that it could be said to be already here. Weiss' contemporary Wilhelm Wrede (1859–1906) questioned whether Mark's Gospel provided the facts of Jesus' life and teaching uninfluenced by Mark's own beliefs, and he taught that Jesus believed that the Kingdom of God lay in the near future, that he himself had to prepare the way for it and that Jesus demanded a very high standard of ethics as preparation for the arrival of the Kingdom.

Albert Schweitzer (1875–1965), in *The Mystery of the Kingdom of God* (1901) and *From Reimarus to Wrede* (1906), which was translated into English as *The Quest for the Historical Jesus* in 1910, the year of Robert Flint's death, interpreted the whole of the life of Jesus in terms of 'thoroughgoing eschatology'. According to Schweitzer, when Jesus himself preached repentance because the Kingdom of God is near, and when he sent his disciples out with that message also, he expected the Kingdom of God to erupt into history very soon. Jesus' ethical teaching applied only to the brief time remaining before the Kingdom arrived. When the Kingdom did not come, Schweitzer's Jesus decided he had to force God's hand by going to Jerusalem to die in order to provoke God into establishing His Kingdom, which would be identical to the Church which Jesus said would be founded on Peter and the gates of hell would not prevail against it.

Robert Flint and Albert Schweitzer could not be further apart in their attitude to the Gospels or their understanding of the Kingdom. What they had in common, however, was that both men reached a view of the Kingdom of God when very young and held to it firmly throughout their life. It was when he was nineteen and on military service that Schweitzer read the tenth chapter of Matthew's Gospel, which describes Jesus sending out his disciples. Schweitzer later wrote:

> In the address with which he sent them out Jesus promised them that they would undergo persecution. This however did not happen. He proclaimed to them that the Son of Man would come before they had completed their journey through the cities of Israel, which could only mean that with his coming the supernatural Messianic Kingdom would be established. He therefore did not expect them to return.[25]

Schweitzer's reading of the text convinced him that events had proved Jesus wrong. All his later writings follow from that moment on military service in Guggenheim. The New Testament scholar Norman Perrin comments that this is both Schweitzer's strength and weakness.[26] Because his insight came to him almost as a revelation he was able to convey it powerfully, but because it came when he was young, his later studies of the New Testament were dominated by it. Robert Flint was in the first year of ordained ministry in Aberdeen, and only in his early twenties, when he preached the sermons that were to be the basis of his understanding of the Kingdom of God which remained unaltered despite the growth of even moderate New Testament scholarship, which made some of his conclusions at least questionable if not unsustainable.

Flint's understanding of the Kingdom of God is open to a number of other criticisms. It is not always clear what the difference is between the Church and the Kingdom. It is not clear in what way the state, science, literature and the arts, by freeing themselves from the control of the Church, have led to the growth of the Kingdom of God. Flint simply makes the general comment that 'when their aims are good and holy, they are no less of the Kingdom of God than [the Church] is'.[27] In his sermon and lectures on the parable of the mustard seed, Flint talks about 'the evolution' of God's Kingdom, but when he illustrates its evolution the examples he uses are 'the evolution of doctrines' and 'systems of theological science'.[28] In other words, the Kingdom's evolution is defined in terms of the Church's doctrinal development.

It is also unclear whether Flint regards the Kingdom as an objective reality which is achievable in human society or as a way of describing subjective religious motivation. He talks about the Kingdom working in the hearts of individuals and about changes in society which bring the Kingdom closer being brought about by complete changes in the human heart. His insistence, however, on the separation of Church and Kingdom implies that the Kingdom has a form of existence similar to that of the Church. Further, he uses the language of the Kingdom not only to describe people's motives for improving social conditions, but the improvements themselves. For example, he told a Church Congress that when there are no more one-apartment houses, God's Kingdom will have made a perceptible advance, and he refers to the state's involvement in education and health as objective evidence of the Kingdom's growth.[29]

Flint advised the Church to recognise that the social question is extremely complex and that social problems cannot be solved in isolation but only with reference to each other. He pointed to the contribution that activities and agencies beyond the Church make towards the Kingdom, which will 'come in all directions', and said that the social problem, as well as being a religious one,

> is also an economic, political, moral and educational one; by no means a religious one, but inclusive of all secular agencies, institutions and movements. The Kingdom of God being thus comprehensive, the attitude of the church to all movements for the amelioration of man's lot should correspond to it.[30]

However, he said that the Church's responsibility is greater because 'the solution of the social problem revealed to her is not one solution among many but the solution, the one which excludes nothing that is true, and includes nothing that is false in other solutions which have been proposed'. That seems remarkably like insisting that other political, economic and social responses to the problem are of value only insofar as they agree with the religious solution, which, as Flint puts it, 'is not one solution among many but is the solution'.[31]

One of the reasons why Flint's first book and his views on the Kingdom of God have been largely ignored is that his later works on theism and anti-theistic theories engaged much more discussion. The influence and effect of his view of the Kingdom of God on his philosophy of history should not be ignored, however. In a passage in his first series of Baird Lectures on theism which has been noted by A. P. F. Sell and the contemporary theologian John Hick, Flint wrote:

> Due weight ought also to be given to the circumstance that the system of God's moral government of our race is only in course of development. We can see but a small part of it, for the rest is as yet unresolved. History is not a whole, but the initial or preliminary portion of a process which may be of vast duration, and the sequel of which may be far grander than the past has been. That portion of the process which has already been accomplished,

small though it be, indicates the direction which is being taken; it is, on the whole, a progressive movement; a movement bearing humanity towards truth, freedom and justice. Is it scientific, or in any wise reasonable, to believe that the process will not advance to its legitimate goal? Surely not.[32]

In *Agnosticism*, Flint describes the philosophical study of history as seeking 'to show that the goal of the evolution of life, so far as it has yet proceeded, is the perfecting of human nature, and the eternal source of things, a power which makes for truth and righteousness'.[33] This understanding of history is entirely consistent with the view of the Kingdom of God that Flint outlined over forty years earlier when he expressed confidence in the continuous progress towards the Kingdom of God in his sermon on the parable of the mustard seed:

> We may fail to measure its progress from day to day, because it is not rapid but slow, not with observation, but without it. We may be unable to detect that a plant which we looked upon yesterday is larger today than it was then, but a month hence the evidences of increase will probably be abundant – and if not, at least a year hence. Still more may we be unable to trace the growth of the Kingdom of God if we limit our scrutiny to a short period or a narrow one, although a more comprehensive view will clearly show that growth has been going on without interruption. The life to which it is due has remained ever identical with itself, casting off what is false and imperfect, but preserving and unfolding what is true and essential.[34]

Whatever criticisms may be made of Flint's view of the Kingdom of God, it initiated the interplay of social theology and the practical work of the Presbyterian Churches in the half century that followed the publication of *Christ's Kingdom upon Earth*. Flint provided the model that enabled the successors in the west of Scotland of Brewster and Burns, Buchanan and Norman Macleod to find a place for social, municipal and statutory responses to the urban crisis in their social theology. His insistence on the separation of Church and Kingdom enabled the Churches no longer to regard social improvements as dependent on religious commitment. His plea to include the work of secular agencies and movements in the work of the Kingdom of God allowed the Churches to regard other parts of civic society as partners, whose efforts were not to be feared as marginalising the Church's role. The work of the Presbytery of Glasgow in the field of Glasgow's slum housing depended on the new paradigm of the Kingdom of God which Robert Flint provided.

NOTES

1. Macmillan, Donald (1914) *The Life of Robert Flint* (London: Hodder and Stoughton), p. 93.
2. Oakley, Charles (1946) *The Second City* (Glasgow: Blackie & Son), p. 68.
3. Renan, Ernest (1935) *Life of Jesus* (London: Watts), p. 85.
4. MacEwan, Alexander (1895) *Life and Letters of John Cairns DD, LLD* (London: Hodder and Stoughton), pp. 463ff.
5. Flint, *Christ's Kingdom upon Earth*, p. 85.
6. Ibid. p. 157.
7. Maurice, F. D. (1966) 'Christmas Day and other sermons', in A. Vidler, *F. D. Maurice and Company* (London: SCM), p. 123.
8. Davies, W. Merlin (1964) *An Introduction to F. D. Maurice's Theology* (London: SPCK), p. 123.
9. Flint, *Christ's Kingdom upon Earth*, p. 189.
10. Ibid. pp. 64–5, 69.
11. Ibid. p. 71.
12. Ibid. p. 71.
13. Flint Papers, New College Library, MSS FLI 1–3.
14. Flint, Robert (1899) *Sermons and Addresses* (Edinburgh: William Blackwood & Sons), p. 52.
15. Ibid. p. 25.
16. Ibid. pp. 34, 36.
17. Flint, Robert (1905) *On Theological, Biblical and Other Subjects* (Edinburgh: William Blackwood & Sons), pp. 243–74.
18. Reid, H. M. B. (ed.) (1899) *First Church Congress, Official Report of Proceedings* (Edinburgh: J. Gardner Hitt), pp. 77–92.
19. Cooper, James (1835) *Disestablishment and Disendowment Contrary to Holy Scripture* (Aberdeen: John Rae Smith), p. 5.
20. Cooper, James (1895) *The Revival of Church Principles in the Church of Scotland* (Oxford: Mowbray & Co.), p. 5.
21. Cooper, James (1898) *The Church Catholic and National* (Glasgow: James Maclehose & Sons), p. 4.
22. Candlish, James (1884) *The Kingdom of God* (Edinburgh: T. & T. Clark), p. 201.
23. Bruce, Alexander B. (1889) *The Kingdom of God* (Edinburgh: T. & T. Clark).
24. Ibid. p. 93.
25. Perrin, Norman (1963) *The Kingdom of God in the Teaching of Jesus* (London: SCM), p. 32.
26. Ibid.
27. Flint, *Christ's Kingdom upon Earth*, p. 70.
28. Ibid. p. 164.
29. Reid, *Official Report of the First Church Congress*, p. 90.

30. Flint, *Christ's Kingdom upon Earth*, p. 83.
31. Ibid. p. 80.
32. Sell, A. P. F. (1987) *Defending and Declaring the Faith: Some Scottish Examples, 1860–1920* (Exeter: Paternoster Press), pp. 60–1; Hick, John (1968) *Evil and the God of Love* (London: Macmillan), pp. 258–9.
33. Flint, Robert (1903) *Agnosticism* (New York: Charles Scribner's Sons), p. 653.
34. Flint, *Christ's Kingdom upon Earth*, pp. 166–7.

3

The Church and Housing

Robert Flint's Social Theology put into Practice

If we are entering on this battle against the evils of society for the object
merely of getting our Churches filled and our Church statistics run up ...
we will fail, and deservedly fail.

Donald Macleod, 1889

In 1888, six million people visited an exhibition of science and art, held in
Glasgow between May and November, opened by the Prince and Princess of
Wales and twice visited by Queen Victoria. The exhibition, which occupied
sixty-four acres of land in the city's West End, was held for two main reasons:
to emphasise Glasgow's imperial status and municipal achievements, and to
raise money for an art gallery and museum to house the city's considerable
collections. In conjunction with the exhibition, the city also hosted meetings
of the British Medical Association, the British Archaeological Association,
the Library Association and the Institute of Naval Architects. In the same
year as the exhibition, the Church of Scotland's Presbytery of Glasgow set up
a Housing Commission to investigate living conditions in the slum properties
of which the six million visitors to the showcase exhibition doubtless saw
little. Conditions in some areas of Glasgow were appalling. Very little light
made its way into the houses. Walls were damp, roofs leaked, staircases and
passages were dilapidated, ventilation was utterly inadequate and the air
was rancid from inefficient drains. Families lived and slept in one room and
siblings slept with parents. Of all the children who died in Glasgow before
the age of five, 32 per cent died in one-roomed houses compared with 2 per
cent in five-roomed houses. Children were at risk from sexual exploitation,
and incest was common.

In the late 1860s a City Improvement Trust began clearing the
dilapidated and insanitary buildings in the East End, expecting that private
enterprise would encourage the regeneration of the area by buying land and
building new houses and business premises. With the collapse of the property
market and the dramatic failure of the City of Glasgow Bank in 1878,
however, builders were no longer willing to buy or feu land, and properties

purchased for demolition and redevelopment were left standing. By 1888 activity in the housing market had resumed, and in six years almost all the land purchased through the City Improvement Trust had been built on and the population around the centre of the old city had dropped by 50,000. A difference had been made to a relatively small area. This was the moment when the Presbytery of Glasgow, led by three city ministers, John Marshall Lang, Donald Macleod and Frederick Lockhart Robertson, started to address the issue of slum housing.

REVD DR JOHN MARSHALL LANG AND REVD DR DONALD MACLEOD

John Marshall Lang had been minister of the Barony parish since 1873. He was a towering figure in the Church of his day at home and abroad, a high churchman and in 1893 Moderator of the General Assembly. Born in 1834, Lang studied at Glasgow University. In 1856 he became minister of the East Church in Aberdeen, but a period of ill health forced him to leave after only two years for the rural parish of Fyvie. In 1865 he moved to the newly created parish of Anderston in Glasgow, then, after three years, to Morningside in Edinburgh and finally to the Barony. He oversaw the building of a new church on a site opposite Glasgow Cathedral. Although the civil parish of the Barony was huge, it was divided among several congregations. The parochial area for which John Marshall Lang was responsible when he went to the Barony was 27,475 and there were 1,945 members of the congregation. When he left in 1900, to become Principal of the University of Aberdeen, the parochial area had grown to around 30,000 and the congregation had increased to 2,292. His son, Cosmo Gordon Lang, who became Archbishop of Canterbury, described his father as a liberal evangelical whose religion was the inspiration of his life.

Donald Macleod was the much younger brother of Norman. He was born in 1831 and studied at Glasgow University. After an assistantship with his brother in the Barony he was inducted to the Borders parish of Lauder in 1858, then to Linlithgow in 1862, and finally became minister of the Park Church, then on the western outskirts of the city, in 1868. By 1868 the population of Park's parish was 7,538 and there were 789 communicant members of the congregation. When Macleod left in 1905 the congregation had grown to 901. It was the wealthiest congregation in Glasgow, the only one whose givings exceeded £5,000. Macleod retired in 1905. He was chaplain to three monarchs and Moderator of the General Assembly in 1895. The *Glasgow Herald* recorded on the day following his death in 1916 that 'no great public monument in the Church or in the city was considered complete without his influence and co-operation'.[1]

The two men were good friends and neighbours in Woodlands Terrace, and their families saw a good deal of each other. Cosmo Gordon Lang said that from his childhood he had a great affection for Donald Macleod. Both men had been contemporaries of Robert Flint at Glasgow University. Flint succeeded Donald Macleod as missioner and then assistant minister to Norman Macleod. He coupled Macleod's *Church and Society*,[2] which contains his social theology in a series of sermons on the Kingdom of God, with Brooke Foss Westcott's earlier *Social Aspects of Christianity*, saying that the two works

> are greatly more valuable than they would have been if their authors had shown a less exquisite sense of knowing always where to stop; and such a sense, only attainable in due measure by assiduous thoughtfulness, is probably even more necessary in addressing congregations composed more of the poor and labouring classes than those which meet in Westminster Abbey or the Park Church.[3]

Marshall Lang will have been well aware of the impact of Robert Flint's sermons on the Kingdom of God. Flint and Marshall Lang were both members of the General Assembly's Home Mission Committee under Donald Macleod's convenership. Both men clearly had sufficient links with Flint to justify the presumption that Flint had considerable influence on their social theology.

Marshall Lang's Baird Lectures, *The Church and its Social Mission*,[4] surveyed the history of the Church's social teaching from Jesus until the author's own day and then examined what, for Marshall Lang, were the primary social issues: the extent of poverty and the 'threat' of socialism and some reactions to them, secular and Christian. Like Flint, Marshall Lang was extremely critical of socialism both on economic grounds and for its lack of a religious impetus without which both Flint and Marshall Lang believed it was deficient. Twice Marshall Lang acknowledged that he was drawing on arguments advanced by Flint: once when Flint dismissed definitions of socialism such as 'every aspiration towards the amelioration of society' as largely meaningless; and again when Flint criticised socialism because

> it leaves out of account God and divine law, sees in morality simply a means to generate happiness, and recognises no properly spiritual and eternal life. It conceives of the whole duty of mankind as consisting in the pursuit and production of social enjoyment. Hence its ideal of the highest good, and consequently of human conduct, is essentially different from the Christian ideal, and thus it necessarily comes into direct conflict with Christianity.[5]

Just as Flint insisted that when the Gospel changes human hearts then the result is a complete change in society, so Marshall Lang wrote, 'A regenerated society means regenerated persons; persons with a right spirit in whom there is a supreme power making the life consistent.'[6] Like Flint he separated Church and Kingdom and saw history as progressive development. He agreed with Flint that the periods when the Church exercised power were when the cause of the Kingdom advanced least. Marshall Lang shared Flint's view of history, that 'all that is true and healthy is ever struggling upwards to complete realisation'.[7] They were both convinced that the Church was least faithful to its commission when it was powerful, and the Church, as Marshall Lang put it, 'in borrowing the clothes of the Empire, exchanged the imperialism of truth for that of worldly power'.[8] They agreed that the Kingdom and the Church are not identical. Marshall Lang wrote that the Kingdom of God

> is not an exclusive Church-State. It is not a State with such distinct political outlines that men shall be able to explain 'Lo, it is there!'. Neither is it a mere hazy cloudland. But it is free from the complications of human governments and ambitions. It is an ethical commonwealth, descending from God out of heaven, that it may pervade and sanctify and enrich all nations and people in all their life. It is to take shape in his Church, though, in its full and proper glory it transcends the Church.[9]

This is hardly as strong as Flint's (and later Donald Macleod's) vigorous repudiation of any identification of Church and Kingdom, and Marshall Lang was less enthusiastic about regarding endeavours outside the Church as contributing towards the coming Kingdom. He acknowledged that 'the motive of much of the humanitarian effort of the day is not a distinctively Christian motive' and that 'men and women realise the characteristic forces of religion, [and] find a religion for themselves, in their idealisations, their art, their science, their work'. He believed, however, that those whose motives were not distinctively Christian were nevertheless unconsciously influenced by Christian thought, though a Christian commitment would give their scientific and artistic interests a richness their secular endeavours lacked.[10] Flint had written that 'to set up the Kingdom of God is indeed to plant churches, but to do vastly more than that – even to alter the whole dispositions and activities of a people',[11] and Marshall Lang too was concerned not with 'ecclesiastical constitution and history, but the social service of the Christian collectivism … the betterment of the individual as well as of society'.[12] Marshall Lang's debt to Flint is considerable.

Donald Macleod's social theology, as well as being contained in the five sermons on the Kingdom of God in *Church and Society*, is also expressed in his editorship of *Good Words*, which he used as a vehicle both for himself and for the contributors whom he chose to express his social theology, which owed even more to Robert Flint than did that of his friend and neighbour

John Marshall Lang. Macleod's understanding of the Kingdom of God reflected Flint's view of it. He echoed Flint's view that the Kingdom of God was not given the place in contemporary thought that it had in the Bible. Both men believed that science, religion and the history of civilisation testified to progress towards the attainment of an ideal human society, a movement, as often unconscious as it was conscious, towards the establishment of the Kingdom of God on earth. Just as Flint saw that evolutionary growth implied 'increasing divergence and definiteness of parts and functions'[13] and thus preserved individuality, so Macleod recognised the element of diversity produced by the seed-like principle of the Kingdom of God, which means that 'the individual retains his natural characteristics; he continues to be imaginative or intellectual, clever or the reverse'.[14]

Flint and Macleod both illustrated their common understanding of the Kingdom by referring to the incarnation and the pattern of Jesus' life. Dealing with the parable of the mustard seed, Flint referred to the 'unobtrusiveness of Jesus and his poverty, sorrows and suffering' as 'the little seed-corn which had to be dropped into the ground and die ere the earth could bear a harvest of righteousness and peace'.[15] Macleod said of Jesus that:

> He had come to bestow a new life, to implant principles, to give vitality to the diviner part that is in man, and through the growth of this life from within, outward confusion would gradually change into order, the law of God would become the law of heart and life, until the glory and goodness which dwelt in Himself would be reflected in humanity, and the reign of God be established in conscience and will.[16]

That the two men should use the incarnation as illustrative of the parables in which Jesus referred to the growth of the Kingdom from unpromising beginnings, and as evidence of that principle at the heart of their understanding of the Kingdom of God, shows the extent of Flint's influence on Macleod.

Macleod and Flint also made use of evolution in how they saw the Kingdom developing. Flint wrote:

> From first to last, from the beginning of human history until now, the immense majority of our race have set before them ends of their own, narrow and mean schemes merely for personal good; and yet although it has been so, and in the midst of confusion, tumult and war, the progress, order, plan I speak of has been slowly and silently but surely built up.[17]

Forty years later Macleod wrote:

> The true measure of the advance of his Kingdom, as distinct from any ecclesiasticism, is to be found in the extent to which the spirit of Christ is

carried into every sphere of interest and duty. For while modern society is certainly to some extent chargeable with such breaches of Christ's law as have been sketched, yet were society resolved into its component parts we would discover a great deal that is apparently sincerely religious in the individuals who compose it.[18]

Macleod and Marshall Lang are frequently cited as together being responsible for the change in the Church of Scotland's attitude to social questions.[19] They both recognised the extent of poverty within the city of Glasgow, for which they used the same image of the upas tree, which, according to legend, was believed to have the power to destroy other growing things within a radius of fifteen miles. They disagreed, however, sometimes publicly and sharply, about whether intemperance was the cause or the consequence of poverty. Macleod's view was expressed in a powerful passage in a speech he made to the General Assembly of 1888 which requires full quotation not only to convey a sense of Macleod's use of vivid imagery, but because the images he employed in this speech he was to use several times in expressing his sympathy for the man and, very significantly, the woman who found release in drink, for which so many churchmen condemned them.

Think of the life of many a working man, coming home from his day's hard labour, tired and depressed, to one of these houses. It may be that the wife has a washing, and the atmosphere is full of the steam of the washing tub, and of the clothes hung up to dry, and she, poor soul, is perhaps irritable and tired also; the children, as children always are, are noisy and restless; the baby, whom the mother scarcely has time to attend, crying and fretful in the cradle. What can a man in these circumstances do? Do you expect every evening the sweet picture presented of the book taken down to read, and a recreation in the one-roomed house of 'The Cotter's Saturday Night'? Alas! The room up several stairs in a close in Glasgow is a different affair from the cottage in Ayrshire, amid fresh air and a thousand outside beauties. Where is the man to go for relaxation, or rather for escape from the state of things I have pictured? If he goes to the 'close-mouth' or to the street to smoke his pipe, he is met by the chill air of the foggy frosty night and an atmosphere laden with the smoke and fumes of manufactories. Where is any resource to be found? Need I answer? The only resource he finds is too frequently the public house. Or I ask you to imagine the life of the labouring man's wife? She may be, as many of them are, a woman who has been trained to method and system, and who can make the fireside bright for her husband; but how many of these poor mothers, with the very best intentions, have not been so trained? They are overwhelmed with toil – children to clothe, babies to feed, houses to tidy, the washing, cooking and the thousand little economies of one who has to manage a little wage, making it meet house-rent, school-fees, and a thousand petty expenses – these accumulating a burden of care upon what is often a feeble frame and nervous temperament, produce naturally prostration and despair, and a craving for anything which will break up the monotony of ceaseless activity, and afford some stimulus and excitement to raise her, even momentarily, above herself. She is also led to the terrible resource of strong drink. Fathers and brethren, you remember the story of Bunyan, who when he saw the man brought to execution, said 'There goes John Bunyan, but for the grace of God'. Dare we, as we contemplate the trials of our poorer brethren, and the sins of intemperance into which they are so often betrayed, assume the Pharisaic attitude of those who thank God that they are not as those who have so fallen in the battle of life. Nay, rather but for the grace of God and for the circumstances in which by his mercy we have been placed, would we be better than they?[20]

In a debate in the General Assembly of 1889, Macleod spoke again of his belief that intemperance was often an attempt to escape from the reality of poverty. Marshall Lang challenged him and

thought the order might be inverted, and that it might be said that poverty was caused by intemperance … He thought that if they were to lock up the public houses, they would remove a large amount of temptation which surrounded the poorer classes

Macleod's retort to this was that 'it was all very well to say "shut up the public houses" but did anyone fancy for a moment that intemperance could be cured by that?'[21] Marshall Lang was as inclined to stress the significance of intemperance as a cause of poverty as Macleod was to minimise it. In a debate in the 1891 Assembly Macleod referred to 'the evil effects of over-crowding and to the way in which drinking habits followed upon the misery of the home', whereas Marshall Lang insisted that everywhere

there stalked the giant form of intemperance. Again and again they were told that the Church, or any philanthropic society might do what they liked, but so long as they had a public house for every 120 or 160 of the population, their work would be useless.[22]

The greatest difference in emphasis between Marshall Lang and Donald Macleod was in what they thought social reform was to achieve. In a sermon to the Synod of Glasgow and Ayr, Marshall Lang made it clear in the text he chose, 'they need not depart',[23] that his aim was simply the evangelical one of encouraging a return to the Church. Speaking to the 1889 General Assembly, he said that

he believed that the cause of non-Church-going was to be found as much in the Church as in the social surroundings. He believed that it was not so

much the masses who had forsaken religion, as religion that had not gone to
the masses.[24]

Again, Marshall Lang's emphasis differed from Macleod's, who said at the
same Assembly that 'he would like to get the opinion of the people, of
working men, on the subject of non-Church-going':[25]

> If we are entering on this battle against the evils of society for the object
> merely of getting our Churches filled and our Church statistics run up; if in
> going to the people we give them the slightest suspicion that the chief end
> we have in view is to get them to go 'to our Church', we will fail and
> deservedly fail.[26]

It is true that Macleod went on to say that it should be irrelevant which
church people go to, but in his emphasis he envisaged a wider social
purpose: 'that we, as a National Church, care chiefly for the good of the
nation; that we desire "not to be ministered unto but to minister"'.[27]

The difference in emphasis in the two men's ways of describing the
Kingdom is also reflected in the way they wrote about it. Marshall Lang saw
the Kingdom of God in wide, sweeping terms, and so his social theology was
similarly inclusive and expressed in broad generalisations. Donald Macleod
believed that good must be done in minute particulars, and so the articles
he commissioned for *Good Words*, and those he wrote himself, reflected a
view of the Kingdom of God advancing slowly by the sort of small steps of
which the material in *Good Words* is a practical example. At the beginning
of his editorship, Donald Macleod continued the rather couthy, kailyard style
that Norman favoured, but by 1880 Donald had begun to introduce more
socially relevant stories into the magazine and more social commentary.
Contributions on social issues that Donald Macleod introduced fall into
two categories: those expressing very general views on the need for social
involvement by Church and individuals, and those providing information
on or descriptions of specific social projects or problems, mostly reflecting
a contributor's personal knowledge or experience.

A number of points may be made about Donald Macleod's editorial
role. First, articles on projects to alleviate the conditions of the poor, or
proposals for the improvement of society's provision for the poor were, for
Macleod, examples of 'the spirit of Christ' working in the world towards
the coming of the Kingdom. Second, they conformed to Macleod's conviction
that contributions made in the secular world had their own integrity and
validity with regard to the coming of the Kingdom of God and did not
require some ecclesiastical or biblical connection. And third, they were
consistent with Macleod's own narrative and descriptive style. He was
ahead of his time in recognising that stories by and about the poor are as

important in advancing the Kingdom of God as objective and intellectual analysis of the problem of poverty.

Macleod was prepared to be far more critical of the Church than Marshall Lang. Social theology played a far greater part in Macleod's overall theological outlook than it did in Marshall Lang's, and Marshall Lang's liturgical interests were never shared by Macleod.

> Those very Christians who, within the sphere of 'religion' busy themselves with ecclesiasticisms and theologies, or theories and signs of Salvation, have all the while, in other spheres, fought and do fight a continual battle against God, and conduct social, commercial and political life on principles which are in direct antithesis to the laws of Christ's Kingdom.[28]

As well as claiming that society is founded on selfishness, Macleod blamed its ills on

> Christians who go to churches and repeat creeds, and are more or less busy about the redemption of their own souls [but] have scarcely ever attempted to bring into play the mighty spiritual powers which God has armed them with, and commanded them to employ; and ... have consistently and continually fought against his laws, and done just the very opposite of what Jesus Christ set forth as the rules of his Kingdom.[29]

He insisted that

> it would be no exaggeration were the words 'social inequality' written over the doors of the vast majority of our Protestant Churches, so exclusively do they seem to be reserved for people who are 'better off' or those at least who can appear there in 'Sunday clothes'.[30]

In the light of passages such as these, it is remarkable that, given the extremely well-off congregation to whom these sermons were preached, Macleod could dedicate *Christ and Society* to it 'in affectionate remembrance of a ministry of nearly twenty four years, during which, owing to the kindness of its members, not an incident has occurred to mar a harmony characterised by perfect confidence and warm personal friendship'.[31]

Both Macleod and Marshall Lang accepted without question both of Flint's views that were crucial for the interplay between social theology and the Church's practical work in the late nineteenth century. Just as Flint referred to the Kingdom being advanced by the secular as well as the sacred, so Macleod criticised religion for hiding behind conventional distinctions between the two and for failing to see the contributions of what he called the Kingdoms of commerce, science, literature and art to the advancement of the Kingdom of God. Similarly, Marshall Lang stressed the contribution of philanthropists, educationists, and local and national politicians to the work of the Kingdom by reducing evil, though their contributions were the greater, he believed, when they had a religious motivation. Both men, however, were unwilling to abandon the traditional view that the Church's role was crucial to the improvement of social conditions, particularly in the field of housing. Macleod spoke about social problems having a solution at the hands of the Christian Church. Marshall Lang held on to the belief that while environmental conditions were a significant factor in deprivation, no permanent improvement would take place without the moral dynamic that Christianity especially contemplated.

While both men owed a great deal to Robert Flint, and their role as leaders in the Church gave them opportunities to promote vigorously a social theology largely derived from Flint, neither of them was prepared to put Flint's social theology rigorously into practice with the same enthusiasm as Frederick Lockhart Robertson. The Housing Commission set up by the Presbytery of Glasgow owed more to the practical expression of Flint's social theology by Robertson than it did to the efforts of Marshall Lang and Donald Macleod.

REVD FREDERICK ROBERTSON AND THE HOUSING COMMISSION

After ministries in Bonhill and Greenock, Frederick Lockhart Robertson became minister of St Andrew's Parish in Glasgow in 1873. This was the Church of Scotland parish that contained the worst housing conditions in the city's East End. Robertson described himself as 'the minister of the Saltmarket'. Initially his strategy was to restore the fabric and interior of St Andrew's in order 'to drag these human beings out of the filthy dens in which they live, and place them in a clearer atmosphere, and in this way imbue them with some sense of the love and greatness and majesty of God'.[32] Interestingly, he saw the Church's role as being aesthetically as well as socially significant. He discovered, however, that the restored St Andrew's was not a place where the poor felt comfortable. Like Norman Macleod before him he preached to his congregation in the forenoon and held evening services for those who lived in the slums of the parish, but evening worship did not have the effect for which he had hoped. So Robertson turned to a different strategy. He employed assistants at his own expense to undertake parish pastoral work and followed Flint's principle of involvement with secular agencies in the service of the larger Kingdom of God. When the City of Glasgow Bank collapsed in 1878, it was Robertson who moved that the bank should be wound up, and he proposed the establishment of the relief fund which was set up. His speech reflected a serious commitment to secular involvement as a way of advancing the Kingdom of God:

I shall, saving my sacred office, divest myself of every other duty and trust, and devote my time and attention to forwarding the success of such a scheme, believing that in doing my humble duty to lessen the appalling pressure of this calamity on many sorrowing hearts, I am serving my Maker and my Master just as truly and well as when I am preaching the blessed Gospel.[33]

Robertson took a keen interest in education. When an Act of parliament made it possible for the profusion and variety of bequests providing for educational provision in the city to be rationalised, it was Robertson who produced the scheme that combined the bequests into three trusts, and he became the first secretary of them. He also became secretary of the Association for the Promotion of Art and Music in Glasgow which administered the funds left over from the Glasgow Exhibition of 1888. Although complaints were made to the Presbytery about Robertson neglecting his work with the church, his commitment to engagement with the secular life of the city was thoroughly consistent with Robert Flint's social theology.

Robertson's crucial involvement with the appointment and work of the Commission set up by the Presbytery of Glasgow to examine housing conditions in the city similarly reflected Flint's views. In April 1888, the Presbytery discussed presenting an overture to the General Assembly.[34] The overture blamed lack of church attendance on poor housing in general and insanitary conditions in particular, as well as intemperance and the absence of educational and social facilities. It proposed that the Assembly should ask its Committees on Home Mission and Life and Work to consider ways of improving church attendance through 'fresh Christian methods along with the efficient working of the parochial system'. In a move that again shows the influence of Flint, Lockhart Robertson proposed that instead the Presbytery should consult with people of knowledge and experience in the fields of housing, public health and the City Improvement Trust to find out how 'the work of the church may be brought into harmonious action with the work of the magistrates, for improving the dwellings and the social and moral habits of the people'. He said to the Presbytery that if it

> transmitted the overture it was admitting that it was at its wits' end, and the Assembly would simply remit the matter to the Home Mission Committee, the bulk of whose members were country parsons, who did not know one tenth of the conditions of the problem that members of the Presbytery knew themselves. The Presbytery decided in favour of the overture which the General Assembly subsequently approved.[35]

The Presbytery of Glasgow met in conference session in December 1888 to discuss two issues: how to reduce the evils of intemperance and improve the social and physical conditions of the poor, and how the worship of the Church might be made more influential. In fact the Presbytery spent all the time available discussing housing conditions and had to postpone the discussion on worship. At this meeting Robertson was successful in asking the Presbytery to set up a Commission to look into housing conditions. He argued very strongly that the Commission should consist not only of members of the Presbytery, but also of others with expertise who could establish whether it was poverty, or something more than poverty, that led people to live in some of the conditions that existed in the city. He agreed to an important suggestion from Marshall Lang that the Commission should include representatives from the Free Church and the United Presbyterian Church in the city.

This was a very significant debate in the history of the Church of Scotland's response to urban deprivation for a number of reasons. Despite all that the Presbytery was being told, there was still an underlying assumption, in terms both of the motion that was discussed and in the speeches made during the debate, that individual moral failure was the main contributory cause of poor housing conditions. Because the Presbytery appointed a Commission and recognised that there were economic and structural causes of poverty, there has been a tendency to assume wrongly that blaming poor social conditions on personal irresponsibility had been abandoned. It also has to be recognised that while the Presbytery had rightly been praised for its initiative in setting up the Commission, very few of its members expressed the same sort of interest in social questions as did Robertson, Marshall Lang and Macleod. Attendance at meetings that dealt with social issues was poor, and the minutes of Kirk Sessions within the Presbytery show that very little heed was taken of requests from the Presbytery to report on social conditions in the parishes. Because the Commission is always referred to as 'the Presbytery of Glasgow's Housing Commission', greater Presbytery involvement in the work has been assumed than is justified, and the use of the Presbytery's name in the title gives the false impression that the Commission was made up of members of the Presbytery. Crucially, it was not. The Presbytery acknowledged that it required expertise from outside the membership of the Presbytery, and that the ministry did not require to be heavily represented. Of the twenty-five members of the Commission, only seven were ministers, and four of them ministered in parishes with areas of extremely poor housing. There were sixteen laymen on the Commission.[36] It was of considerable significance that the Presbytery which then, as now, was heavily weighted towards the ordained ministry rather than the eldership, chose to give the Commission an overwhelmingly lay, expert majority and to include members from other

Presbyterian denominations. In recognising the contribution towards a more humane society of those who worked in secular employment, and in insisting that the Church's job was to establish facts and present them to those in authority, the influence of Flint through Robertson on the composition and purpose of the Commission is again clear. One of the constant themes of Robert Flint's speeches in the Church conferences was that the Church had always first to establish facts.

The Housing Commission has rightly been praised as marking a considerable development in the Church of Scotland's social theology and action. Two qualifications need to be made, however. First, the schools inspector William Jolly felt it necessary to add a caveat to the report, saying that the Commission had been too influenced by the views of landlord. There is considerable justification for that view. The Glasgow Landowners and House Factors Associations were represented at all the meetings of the Commission. In one session when Councillor William Smith, who was a member of the Town Council's Sanitary Commission, rigorously questioned James Danksen of the Landlords Association, who claimed not to know any landlords who were 'negligent, obstructive and niggardly', Donald Macleod, Marshall Lang and Frederick Robertson all intervened in a way protective of Danksen and critical of Smith. A subsequent letter to the *Glasgow Herald* from J. Shaw Maxwell of Elmbank Crescent claimed that at the Commission's hearings, representatives of factors, feuars and landlords 'had a remarkably fine innings'.[37] Second, the Commission did not entirely avoid the conventional view which attributed pauperism to intemperance, concluding that it was 'strongly impressed with the opinion, stated again and again with precision and distinctness, that drunkenness is the prolific source of the major part of the poverty, wretchedness and discomfort which exist'.[38] This certainly chimed with the views of Marshall Lang but that conclusion was balanced by a reflection of Donald Macleod's opinion that poverty was as serious a cause of intemperance as intemperance was of poverty. The Commission's report stated that

> the preaching of the Word must remain in the forefront, for nothing less potent than the virtue of the divine life can lend strength to the enthralled soul to grapple with the passionate impulses which move it to evil; but, combined with the preaching of the Word there must be wise efforts of a social and economic kind.[39]

From the outset the cost of renting accommodation renovated through the City Improvement Trust concerned the Commission. It was told that in the Saltmarket, property that had been restored under the City Improvement Trust was rented at £8 for a room with a hall and £11 for two rooms, and this was far beyond the means of many. In 1873–4 there had been 12,000 houses available for a rent below £4, and 70,000 under £10; in 1888, there were 7,600 under £4 and 78,000 under £10, an increase of only 8,000, although the population of the city had increased by 80,000. Lockhart Robertson chaired the Housing Commission and it was he who first raised what was to be the Commission's main recommendation: the setting up of an association, supported by public-spirited individuals, to purchase and renovate property which would be available at low rent to the deserving poor. Despite the opposition of land valuators who gave evidence to the Commission and said that an association would not be economically viable, the final report of the Housing Commission concluded that

> an Association could be conducted profitably, on the footing that the properties are acquired at a moderate price; that they are carefully managed; that the tenants are selected, and efforts made to improve their habits and soften their manners, and to encourage them in the way of well-doing, either by caretakers or lady visitors; that properties to be dealt with are situated in localities which workers have selected as most suitable and convenient for their requirements. Tenements of this class could be purchased on moderate terms. An Association holding contiguous blocks could manage them more advantageously than a person owning a single tenement. The Commission are supported in this conclusion by what has been accomplished on a small scale by the proprietors of such tenements.[40]

Robertson presented the Commission's report and findings to the Presbytery in April 1891, and the Commission was given authority to air the issue of housing conditions in a wider context. Robertson organised a meeting of various interested parties, including the Merchants' House and the Trades' House, the Landlords Association and the Charity Organisation Society, as well as representatives of the Free, United Presbyterian and Episcopal Churches. The meeting was chaired by the Lord Provost in early December 1891. It was Robertson once more who introduced the Commission's findings to the meeting and proposed that a wider conference be held to promote agreement on them. The conference was held the following March, and Robertson chaired it. It decided that a public meeting should be held in May in the St Andrew's Halls.

On 13 May 1892 a large public meeting was held in the St Andrew's Halls.[41] Over 100 leading churchmen, industrialists and figures from the city's commercial and public life were on the platform. A large attendance of the public was present to hear the MP, J. G. A. Baird of Gartsherrie, move the motion that an Association for improving the conditions of people by means of labour centres, better housing and recreation be formed. Baird said that as a result of the work of the Presbytery 'we cannot plead ignorance now'. The motion was seconded by Lord Rosebery, who was the principal speaker of the evening. Rosebery, a Liberal imperialist, was widely regarded at the time as the heir apparent to Gladstone. He had already served a short time as Foreign Secretary in Gladstone's third administration and was shortly to do so again in his fourth, and was to serve as Prime Minister from 1894 to 1895. When he spoke to the Glasgow meeting he was Chairman of the London County Council. 'Things are not as they should be anywhere,' Rosebery told the meeting, 'but they are still less well than they should be in Glasgow which has taken the lead in this great municipal movement for the raising of the conditions of the working classes.' He was particularly concerned to stress the high death rate, but added that even worse than the death rate was 'that helpless, hopeless class … which cannot and will not work, and breed a race as shiftless and helpless and degraded as themselves'. Although on this occasion he seems to have succumbed to the popular view, he was not always inclined to do so. For example, in an earlier speech he had 'condemned the puritan obsession with the drinking habits of the working class', perhaps, in part, in an attempt to gain the electoral support of the liquor trade.[42]

Rosebery was followed by Robertson, who addressed his favourite topic of those 'respectable and self-respecting people, many of them fresh from the country, earning sixteen shillings or eighteen shillings a week' and for whom there was no decent housing available. He said that the Churches were working together with the Corporation and civic authorities to organise associations to purchase property, to reconstruct it and to put it in a sanitary condition. Following Robertson's speech Sir William Arroll proposed that the meeting commend the new Association to the liberality of all and ask for pledges of financial support from those who were prepared to be patrons, pledging £100 in the first twelve months, or guarantors for lesser sums, or annual subscribers. Lord Rosebery was elected President of the Association and Dr Flockhart Robertson its Chairman.

Just over six months later, Robertson died. His efforts to seek support for the Church's plan from as wide a representation of the city as possible was clearly inspired by the social theology of Robert Flint, involving as it did cooperation in the promotion of the Kingdom of God, which Flint once said would be advanced when housing conditions in the East End of Glasgow were dramatically improved. Perhaps it is because he did not live, and the work of advocating the improvement of housing within the Church was taken over by Marshall Lang and Donald Macleod in the General Assembly, that the part played by Lockhart Robertson has not been recognised. His name, however, should be linked with those of Marshall Lang and Macleod, as it was in the General Assembly of 1891 when the report of the Presbytery's Housing Commission was laid on the table. It was Robertson who presented the report to the General Assembly. Following speeches by Marshall Lang and Macleod, the Moderator said that very rarely in the history of any Parliament or Convention or Assembly had three more able, more well-informed or more thrilling speeches been made upon a more momentous subject, closely touching the deepest welfare of the Church and the land, than the three addresses to which they had just listened.[43]

The part played by Donald Macleod and John Marshall Lang in awakening the social conscience of the Church of Scotland was extremely significant. Both men were national figures of considerable importance and reputation. Both were to become Moderators of the General Assembly. Macleod was an outstanding preacher and orator and Marshall Lang was a powerful intellectual. They were able, therefore, to command attention and respect for the Housing Commission, and, equally important, for the social theology that lay behind it. Robertson did not possess the oratorical gifts of Donald Macleod or the intellectual credentials of Marshall Lang, but his determination and organisational ability were essential to the Housing Commission's work. The evidence given to the Commission reveals the extent to which Robertson piloted through the proposal for a housing association, which resulted in the Glasgow Workmen's Dwelling Company, with a capital of over £40,000 and a dividend limited to 5 per cent. It bought and renovated twenty-six slum properties and was responsible for erecting six new tenements. Tenants were largely unskilled labourers earning around £1 per week. The Company owned 677 houses providing accommodation for 2,900 people.

THE UNITED FREE CHURCH AND THE MUNICIPAL HOUSING COMMISSION

In 1902, the Lord Provost of Glasgow set up a Municipal Commission into housing conditions in the city. Because of the work already done by its Presbytery's Commission, the Church of Scotland did not give evidence, although several members of the Commission were elders. The view of the Glasgow Presbytery of the United Free Church (formed in 1900 through the union of the Free Church and the United Presbyterian Church) was expressed by two ministers from areas of deprivation, Gilbert Laurie of Fairbairn United Free Church in Bridgeton and William Ross from the Cowcaddens.[44] In several important respects their evidence was very different from the conclusions reached by the Church of Scotland Commission. First, they were much more severely critical of landlords. Laurie condemned over-crowding, citing one tenement occupied by 120 people, and said that rents for property that had deteriorated considerably in the twenty-five years of his ministry in the city had risen sharply. He also criticised landlords for avoiding expense by failing to provide adequate factoring. Ross also condemned the charging of high rents for unhealthy properties and went so far as to suggest that landlords should be made entirely responsible for the good conduct of their tenants. Second, the evidence from the United Free Church was that intemperance lay at the root of the housing problem. It is perhaps not surprising that Ross, who held high office in the temperance movement's Order of Templars, said to the Commission that the principal cause of lamentable conditions was 'drinking customs and the drinking trade'. Laurie's view was similar, though expressed in a rather more balanced way. While he regarded drink as the most powerful element in causing deprivation, he added that 'if you don't put people in a position where they can breathe fresh air, then that can work into drinking'. Third, Laurie and Ross were far more critical of the institutional Church than was the Church of Scotland's Commission. The Church of Scotland Presbytery of Glasgow's Housing Commission barely mentioned any criticism of the Church at all, whereas both Laurie and Ross made a major point of it. Gilbert Laurie said to the Commission that the churches had been failing in their duty by neglecting those in poverty and poor housing. William Ross criticised the Church of Scotland because its congregations would not take the trouble to become involved in social problems, while the United Free Church, 'not supported by the State ... has just enough to do to preserve its own organisation and cannot afford, so to speak, to take the necessary steps to meet the condition of things'. Anything the United Free Church had been able to do had been done, he said, 'by the aid of generous and Christian people who had compassion on that class of the population'. He was particularly scathing about

> west end congregations who play at missions to relieve their own consciences. Their visitors go about, not with the object of raising the community but with the object of doing what they say is Christian work. They pay and provide charity out of pure sympathy without regard to causes, to righteousness or the results, and they make people dependent.[45]

The distinction Ross made between raising the community and Christian work is an important one. He started a medical mission in his church buildings where in ten years over forty thousand people were treated free of charge. His congregation paid for teams of two women to live in slum communities to help individual families improve so that people would move to better areas, and he claimed that this 'pioneer mission' (as he called it) resulted in a frequent turnover of the population. He was involved in campaigning for municipal libraries and savings banks in Cowcaddens.

The fourth area of disagreement between the evidence of the United Free Church to the Municipal Commission and the recommendations of the

Presbytery of Glasgow's Housing Commission was over municipal housing. The Church of Scotland Commission did not make any recommendation about municipal housing, though as we have seen one member of it, William Jolly, entered a caveat expressing regret that the case for municipal housing had not been made. In fact only one person who gave evidence to the Commission, Bruce Glazier, the secretary of the Glasgow branch of the Socialist League, argued for it, as he had done to the Presbytery of Glasgow's Housing Commission. In his evidence William Ross supported the provision of council houses. Gilbert Laurie, sharing the Church of Scotland Commission's concern for those who could not afford housing at an affordable rent, advocated the provision of municipal housing for those who could not afford more than 10 shillings a month in rent. Along with recommendations for the strengthening of the Corporation's powers with regard to overcrowding and the prevention of insanitary premises being occupied, the Municipal Commission recommended that the Corporation build tenements of one or two apartments 'for respectable people of the poorest class', with preference being given to those whose homes had been demolished. The Commission also recommended the provision of simpler, more basic accommodation for those who were considered 'dissolute'.

The Revd Robert Howie, the minister of St Mary's United Free Church in Govan, was a member of the Municipal Commission. Howie made two attempts to have the Commission's eventual findings altered in significant ways, both of which proved unsuccessful. First, he failed to have a recommendation that the Corporation should provide one or two lodging houses in different districts of the city for 'poor couples' altered to include a stipulation that the couples be married. Second, and of greater significance, he failed to persuade the Commission to include a recommendation that it would be preferable to build municipal housing in the suburbs rather than in inner-city areas. When the Commission's final recommendations were being drawn up, Howie asked that his signature should bear a caveat that he approved only with reservations that this proposal had been dismissed as 'irrelevant'. When this was refused, he declined to sign the report.

Robert Howie was someone of considerable ability in the field of statistics. In a letter to the *Glasgow Herald* he argued that the Commission should have paid more attention to the statistics of migration to the suburbs.[46] In the ten years before additional suburban districts were annexed to the city, the population of the city had risen by 10.27 per cent from 565,710 to 623,829. In the same period the population of the suburban areas added had risen by 49.29 per cent from 92,363 to 137,883, and the population of some parishes within Glasgow (Glasgow, Govan, Eastwood, Cathcart and Rutherglen) had dropped by 219,556 or 34.16 per cent. Howie claimed in his letter that if the Corporation secured ground in the suburbs for municipal housing, then the ratepayers and not private landowners would benefit from the increased value of the land which would follow the extension of the tramways system to these areas. The Corporation would therefore be able to build cheaper houses than it could in the inner city, where more existing housing would become available for let as people moved out to the suburbs. Howie produced figures that showed that the demand for larger accommodation within the city was decreasing and was being fully met by private enterprise.

The United Free Church might no longer have statutory territorial responsibilities but its strategy remained committed to the territorial principle. Gilbert Laurie and William Ross articulated the belief that it was through the combined work of ministers and congregations at the local level that the welfare of the city as a whole would be improved. When Gilbert Laurie was asked what the Church could do to help the municipal authorities tackle poor housing conditions, Laurie said that he knew of no other way than by resolutely working with a limited number of people in a local area. He was scathing about the 'imperialistic' approach that tried to tackle social problems and conditions on a city-wide scale. If the Church concentrated on the congregation's local area, then the conditions of people would be improved and their standard of living raised. William Ross was equally dismissive of the involvement of West End congregations in areas of deprivation which he said not only relieved the consciences of the comfortably off but also encouraged a dependency culture in the poor areas: 'They pay for and provide charity out of pure sympathy, without regards to causes, to righteousness or results.' He regarded the work of the City Improvement Trust as disastrous because the Cowcaddens had become the area of choice for those who had been displaced to make way for renovation. The United Free Church was, literally, committed to parochialism. This strategy was not only practically flawed but theologically questionable and constitutionally indefensible. It was practically flawed because it failed to recognise that the social conditions that it believed it could improve required regulation and resources, planning and staffing which could only be provided at the municipal level. It continued to give the Church a key role in improving social conditions at the local level when the resources at that level were insufficient. It was theologically questionable because it assumed a separation between sacred and secular. And it was constitutionally dubious because the United Free Church regarded the Presbytery as the basic unit of the Church's organisation, exercising oversight within a wide area. The very support that wealthier congregations gave to the poorer was intended to be part of the United Free Church's Presbyterian ethos. In effect, however, it operated a congregational ethos, and it was that ethos that was incompatible with Robert Flint's social theology based on the Kingdom of God. It identified

Flint's theology with the Church of Scotland's claim to be the national Church with responsibilities for the welfare of the city. While the Church of Scotland was also tied to its belief in the validity of a territorial ministry, the strategy implicit in its social theology involved regarding society as a whole, and also a commitment to the biblical injunction to 'seek the welfare of the city', a commitment that the United Free Church tended to regard as a form of ecclesiastical imperialism.

NOTES

1. *Glasgow Herald*, 12 February 1916.
2. Macleod, Donald (1893) *Christ and Society* (London: Isbister & Co.).
3. Reid, *Official Report of the First Church Congress*, p. 70.
4. Lang, John Marshall (1892) *The Church and its Social Mission* (Edinburgh: William Blackwood & Sons).
5. Ibid. p. 277.
6. Ibid. p. 274.
7. Ibid. p. 42.
8. Ibid. p. 83.
9. Ibid. p. 28.
10. Ibid. p. 43.
11. Flint, *Christ's Kingdom upon Earth*, p. 71.
12. Lang, *Church and its Social Mission*, p. 13.
13. Flint, *Christ's Kingdom upon Earth*, p. 163.
14. Macleod, *Christ and Society*, p. 89.
15. Flint, *Christ's Kingdom upon Earth*, p. 157.
16. Macleod, *Christ and Society*, p. 89.
17. Flint, *Christ's Kingdom upon Earth*, p. 56.
18. Macleod, *Christ and Society*, p. 9.
19. A. C. Cheyne (1983), in *The Transforming of the Kirk* (Edinburgh: Saint Andrew Press), has written of the late-nineteenth-century Church's willingness to express concern for those he describes as 'at the bottom of the social heap … The outstanding instances of this preparedness probably came from the Auld Kirk's Glasgow Presbytery, where men like Marshall Lang and Donald Macleod brought about a whole series of reports and debates on bad housing and its religious implications.' In a very significant article written in 1977, 'The Churches in Scotland c1870–1900: towards a new social conscience' (*Records of the Scottish Church History Society*, pp. 155–68), Donald Withrington refers to the work of the Church of Scotland's Presbytery of Glasgow, 'led by Lang and Donald Macleod', as illustrating 'the changing climate of the late 1880s' towards social issues. Donald Smith (*Passive Obedience*, pp. 281–2) links the Moderatorial addresses of the two men, Lang's in 1893

and Macleod's in 1895, as displaying 'much more advanced social views' than the addresses of their predecessors who were 'largely unaware of the challenge which the social, political and economic changes of the period presented to the Church'. S. J. Brown, in 'Reform, reconstruction, reaction: the social vision of Scottish Presbyterianism c1830–c1930' (*Scottish Journal of Theology*, vol. 44, 1991, p. 498), describes Macleod and Lang as 'Christian progressives [who] shared a new appreciation for the role of social environment in shaping individual character. They recognised that overcrowding, poor diet, and the drabness of slum life could ensure moral and spiritual defeat for all but the strongest or most fortunate, and that individual vices, especially intemperance, were frequently more the effects than the causes of poverty.'

20. Macleod, Donald (1888) *Non-Church-Going and the Housing of the Poor* (Glasgow: William Blackwood & Sons).
21. *Glasgow Herald*, 1 June 1889.
22. *Glasgow Herald*, 28 May 1891.
23. Lang, John Marshall (1887) *They Need not Depart* (Glasgow: Boyce & Son), p. 4.
24. *Glasgow Herald*, 1 June 1889.
25. Ibid.
26. Ibid.
27. Macleod, *Non-Church-Going*, p. 17.
28. Macleod, *Christ and Society*, p. 34.
29. Ibid. p. 35.
30. Ibid. p. 47.
31. Ibid. Dedication.
32. Thomson, James (1905) *A History of St Andrew's Parish* (Glasgow: Robert Anderson).
33. Ibid. p. 46.
34. Minutes of the Presbytery of Glasgow, 17 April 1888, Strathclyde Regional Archives, CH2/171/25.
35. *Glasgow Herald*, 18 April 1888.
36. W. T. Gairdner was the Professor Emeritus of Medicine at Glasgow University and a former medical officer of health for the city. James Gray was a hatter, J. H. Dickson was a merchant and W. R. W. Smith was a yarn agent. All three, however, were members of Glasgow Corporation. J. Cleland Burns and Leonard Gow were shipowners and W. Graham and Nathaniel Spence were accountants, though Spence resigned from the Commission on moving to London. J. Honeyman was an architect (on whose staff was a young man called Charles Rennie Mackintosh), William Jolly was a schools inspector, David Murray was the Dean of the Faculty of Procurators, A. J. Hunter was Secretary of the Glasgow United Trades' Council, James Parnie was a partner in a firm of accountants and property agents, Sir John Cuthbertson had been MP for

Kilmarnock Burghs and was Chairman of the Glasgow School Board, and William Smart was the first Professor of Political Economy at Glasgow University. William Baird belonged to the family of steel producers.

37. *Glasgow Herald*, 5 February 1890.
38. *Report of the Commission on the Housing of the Poor in Relation to their Social Conditions*, Presbytery of Glasgow, p. 23.
39. Ibid. p. 25.
40. Ibid. p. 21.
41. *Glasgow Herald*, 14 May 1892.
42. McKinstry, Leo (2005) *Rosebery: A Statesman in Turmoil* (London: John Murray), p. 65.
43. *The Scotsman*, 28 May 1891.
44. *Evidence given to Glasgow Municipal Commission on the Housing of the Poor*, pp. 564–80.
45. Ibid. p. 578.
46. *Glasgow Herald*, 1 August 1904.

4

Divisions in the Kingdom
The Extremes of Social Theology

The Church's duty is not to make laws, not to lobby public questions, not to pronounce on the matter of hours and wages, not to play policemen in the streets, but to make men of faith.

William Clow, 1913

In 1909, the General Assemblies of the Church of Scotland and the United Free Church took the first official steps towards reunion. A conference of 210 representatives of the two Churches took place on 9 November 1909. On St Andrew's Day, exactly three weeks after the first meeting of representatives to explore the issues involved in reunion, another conference between the two Churches took place to review their social work. By then, there had already been cooperation between the Churches in the field of social work, for example in response to the welfare needs of those in Glasgow affected by the downturn in trade that year. The Conference showed some concern that there might be a duplication of work, and so it was decided that the Church of Scotland should continue to put its emphasis on practical social work, while the United Free Church should continue the interest it had already expressed in social theology and criticism. The ensuing debate about social theology in the United Free Church was conducted within diverging views about the Kingdom of God. What the United Free Church Assembly was being asked to decide in the opening years of the twentieth century was whether the Church's role in advancing the Kingdom of God was an active participatory one in which the Church provided the means to attempt to reduce poverty and homelessness; or whether it should adopt an inspirationally participative role, working to produce Christian people who would carry the social implications of the Gospel into the places where they had influence; or whether the Church had an institutionally prophetic role, critical of all it regarded as retarding the Kingdom of God. These roles were not, of course, mutually exclusive, and indeed it would have been possible for the Church to adopt all three, but different social theologies often appeared to adopt one of these roles almost at the expense of the others.

In the years leading up to the outbreak of the First World War, Britain faced several crises. Some of them were parliamentary, arising first from the House of Lords' rejection of Lloyd George's 'People's Budget' of 1909 and then from the ensuing conflict between Lords and Commons culminating in the Parliament Act of 1911. Parliamentary conflicts sometimes matter less to the public than those involved in them imagine, but the two elections of 1910, brought about by the constitutional crisis, contributed to a sense of instability in the country. The death of the popular Edward VII and the accession of George V, who was perceived to be much more distant, added a further element of uncertainty. In addition to the destabilising effect of the constitutional crisis there was continuing uncertainty over the future of Ireland as the government introduced a third Home Rule Bill. There was always concern about the future of the north of Ireland in the west of Scotland, but the Irish question posed a wider question for Scotland if, as was claimed, sixty-two of the seventy-two MPs for Scottish constituencies supported Home Rule for Scotland.

From 1905, syndicalists began to urge that trades unions should work towards taking power at local and national levels through federations of unions becoming the local authority for the area, and a national congress of all unions becoming the government. The trades unions' control of different industries would come about, so the syndicalists believed, through a series of strikes, culminating in a General Strike. Those who took the syndicalist threat seriously found a good deal of evidence to justify their fears that there would be strikes in all the major industries after 1910. In 1913 there was a record number of 1,497 strikes, and unemployment rose to 11.3 per cent. Later the same year the Riot Act had to be read in Liverpool and the army was deployed in Liverpool and South Wales.

In addition to the widespread industrial unrest, the 'Women's Revolt' became increasingly militant after 1910, the year in which Emily Davison was arrested attempting to set light to a pillar box in Parliament Street in London with paraffin. The following year stones were thrown at the Prime Minister's windows. In 1913, suffragettes damaged the orchid house in Kew, set fire to a railway carriage and bombed Lloyd George's home. And in that same year Emily Davison threw herself under the King's horse at the Derby.

Just as the United Free Church General Assembly was preparing for an important debate focusing on the Church's understanding of the Kingdom of God, and its attitude to the Church's engagement with social issues, the Glasgow theologian James Denney published an article in *The British Weekly*, one of a series written by him entitled 'The Church and the Kingdom'.[1] Denney castigated those who 'fall back on economical and political questions as though they had a reality which could not be claimed for God and the soul, sin and atonement, death and immorality'. James Denney and his colleague in Trinity College Glasgow, William Clow, are linked in a theological attack within the United Free Church to any social theology that involved political or economic judgements. While there has been a tendency to date the decline of the Churches' engagement with social issues after the First World War, this chapter and the following one trace it to the years before war broke out.

REVD PROFESSOR JAMES DENNEY

James Denney was possibly the most popular minister in the United Free Church of Scotland. Certainly no minister commanded greater respect, and his early death in 1917 at the age of sixty-one was said to have caused consternation in the Church. Speakers in the United Free Church General Assembly for years afterwards expressed regret that the Assembly was deprived of his guidance. Denney was ordained and inducted to Broughty Ferry East Free Church in 1886, succeeding A. B. Bruce. In 1897 he became Professor of Systematic Theology in the Free Church College in Glasgow, and three years later he transferred to the Chair of New Testament Language, Literature and Theology. He became Principal of Trinity College in 1915. Denney had been actively involved in the 1900 union between the Free Church and the United Free Church and was a strong supporter of and involved in the early discussions which led to the reunion of the Churches in 1929. So considerable was his influence that a Church of Scotland minister was said to have insisted that if Dr Denney advocated union there would be union; if Dr Denney was opposed to union there would not be.

Denney was the exception to the widespread acceptance by the beginning of the twentieth century of Flint's dictum that the Church was subordinate to the Kingdom. At the start of the first of his 1909 articles on the Church and the Kingdom in *The British Weekly*, which were published in book form the following year, he attacked

> wild and irresponsible criticism which takes pleasure in asserting that Jesus did not institute the Church and that his whole interest was in the Kingdom of God which is assumed to be a better thing for which the Church will be abandoned'[2]

In the context of discussing worship as the Church's primary function, Denney criticised sermons dealing with questions of economics and politics as an easy option compared to preaching the Gospel. His intention was to show that it was unfaithful to the teaching of Jesus to use the phrase 'the Kingdom of God on earth' to mean a Christianised society, amounting to no more than life as we presently know it, but with the economic and social changes that the Gospel demanded. Jesus' view was that the Kingdom of God was a transcendent Kingdom which will come like a thief in the night, when people least expect it. It cannot therefore be built up by human efforts. The world must wait for it to come in an instant by the decisive intervention of God.

> Nothing could be more remote from [Jesus'] temper than the suggestion that if only all men had their rights – political, economical, educational – the Kingdom would have come. The whole conviction of Jesus about the Kingdom is allied rather to indifference about such things than emphasising their importance. There is a strong tendency to a kind of Christian secularism in much of the labour spent for what is called the Kingdom of God. There is love to men at the heart of it, and in that it comes from Jesus; but in the stress it lays on worldly vocations, in the vast consequences it attaches especially to unfavourable or unfair economic conditions, its connection with Jesus is open to question. The fact is not open to dispute that His conception of the Kingdom of God made Jesus conspicuously indifferent to many things which at present are frequently identified with the Kingdom.[3]

Denney was not opposed to social reform. He simply believed that moves towards it had their own legitimacy. They did not need the endorsement of a very different kingdom and should not usurp its name. His main interest in social reform was in the temperance movement, which, he said, the Church may appropriately support, but may not express a preference between the different political means to promote it. There are good laws and bad laws but when legislation is complete, the whole work of the Church remains to be done. The Church, Denney concluded, would be doing its Christian duty, and serving the state most, if it left legislation to parliament, which is the divine vehicle for ordering the affairs of state. Denney had earlier refused even to allow that the Church might mediate in industrial disputes. In the context of the intervention by the Bishop of Durham, Brooke Foss Westcott, in a miners' strike, Denney said that the Church had no business attempting the understanding of industry necessary to mediation and should confine itself to cultivating among church members the spirit of generosity and humanity.

A recent intellectual and contextual biography of Denney has concluded that Denney was fundamentally averse to the Church making comment on or being involved in political change because of his firm conviction that even if social improvements were desirable, the Church should not be party to the compromises and negotiations that the political process involves. Paradoxically, someone like Denney, who championed the cause of theological freedom to meet contemporary needs, was unwilling to support the systemic social and political changes that would meet the needs of workers and of women.[4]

James Denney's is the clearest and most direct theological attack on the views of Robert Flint, not only on the issues of the separation of Kingdom and Church and the exclusively future and transcendent nature of the Kingdom of God, but also in his absolute refusal to recognise that legislation can play any part in the advancement of the Kingdom. He wrote to Robertson Nicol, who was the editor of *The British Weekly*, in advance of writing his 1909 articles:

> At present I feel very distrustful of the organised action of Churches to promote legislation even for Christian ends, or ends which can be represented as Christian and perhaps if I said what I thought you would feel it is out of keeping with a journal of Christian and social progress. The Church needs to learn that it can help society best by minding its own business and letting the legislature do its.[5]

Before he became involved in the discussions with the Church of Scotland about reunion, Denney was opposed both to Flint's support for what he regarded as the 'fact' of establishment, and to any proposals for Church unity. He described himself in another letter to William Robertson Nicol as sympathetic to Congregationalism.[6]

The 'thoroughgoing eschatology' of Denney's understanding of the Kingdom is certainly in tune with the view expressed by Albert Schweitzer, whose works were translated into English after Denney published his views on the Kingdom. Denney read widely in German theology and would have been aware of Schweitzer's work, though he would not have agreed with Schweitzer's conclusions. There is an element of unfairness, however, in Denney's criticism of those who took a different view of the Kingdom of God. In a letter to Robertson Nicol shortly before the publication of *The Church and the Kingdom*, he accused ministers who were supporting social reform of doing so because they did not believe the Gospel and in order to court popularity. And he repeated that charge publicly. There are also places where Denney takes on the role more of a polemicist than of a New Testament scholar, bearing out J. R. Fleming's description of 'his rather impatient contempt for those who could not view things from his angle'.[7] He virtually ignored all the passages in the Gospels in which Jesus is recorded as having spoken of the Kingdom in the present tense, and appears not even to entertain the possibility that although Jesus had an understanding of the Kingdom coming in the future, his references to it in the present tense can be taken as evidence that he saw his ministry and mission ushering in the age of the Kingdom. When he outlines his stern opposition to any involvement by the Church in legislation, and the limitations of legislation in the long-term improvement of the human condition, Denney makes use of St Paul's comments on the inadequacy of the Mosaic law as a means of salvation. It is hardly legitimate, however, to use Paul's argument against a very specific form of religious legalism in support of his attack on the contemporary use of legislation in the social field.

REVD PROFESSOR WILLIAM CLOW

William Clow was born in Glasgow but received his schooling in New Zealand and the United States and then graduated in arts and divinity from Glasgow University. He was a minister in Lanarkshire, Aberdeen and Edinburgh before being inducted to Stevenson Memorial in the West End of Glasgow in 1902. Later he became Professor of Practical Theology and then Principal of the United Free Church's Trinity College in Glasgow. Clow's social theology is outlined in *Christ and the Social Order*,[8] which was published in 1913, summing up views he had expressed in his pulpit since the date of his induction. The date is significant because it was a year that saw an unprecedented number of strikes.

Clow was a conservative, and his congregation in Glasgow's West End was a comfortable middle-class one, drawn from the terraced houses that had been built to the north of Great Western Road, and the tile-lined red-sandstone apartment blocks of north Kelvinside. It is not difficult to imagine Clow's congregation's anxious response to the growing series of crises that were evidence of the sinful world's need of redemption which was so often the theme of their minister's sermons. Clow regarded the conferences on social and other issues that were held by the United Free Church and the Church of Scotland as of no value. He believed that a minister who wished to follow the prophetic example of Amos or Hosea in making political pronouncements should resign his charge and then devote himself to what he wanted to say, and which Clow admits he would then be entitled to say. Clow took the view, however, that because Presbyteries and the General Assembly are responsible for overseeing the Christian life of members of the Church they may have a responsibility to explore public issues, but only from an ethical standpoint.

> The Church court has a duty of pronouncing upon the ethical import of all proposed legislation, of all civic regulations, and of the administration of the law of the land. It should insist that economics must be ethical. It should insist that laws shall not imperil the liberty of conscience, or the freedom of religion. It should insist that no legislation shall encourage any laxity, or self-indulgence, or discourage the finer instincts of the people. Where there are laws of commerce which break Christ's commandments, where there are customs which injure the young, oppress the feeble, wrong the poor, corrupt

either the minds or the bodies of those who toil, where there are tyrannies of rich over poor, or of poor over rich, where there is any invasion or infringement of ethical righteousness by the laws of the land, or in their administration, there the voice of the Church, by its courts, should never fail to be heard.[9]

That passage illustrates a confusion in Clow's social theology. The passionate rhetoric demanding that the voice of the courts of the Church be heard where there is social injustice is as impressive as that of any who would have regarded themselves as theological critics of Clow. Clow, however, immediately qualified the right he granted to Church courts to speak on political and social issues: 'This voice must speak only within the sphere of ethics, and any heady denunciation of riches as riches, employers as employers, or of workmen as workmen, is an offence against society and against the command of Christ.' He did not recognise that both the use of wealth and the issues surrounding industrial relationships might involve an ethical dimension. He did not appear to realise that when, in his passionate defence of things as they are, he dismissed appeals for shorter working hours as the dignity of idleness replacing the dignity of labour, or when he attacked the reforming legislation of the 1906 Liberal government on old age pensions, national insurance and employment as the results of organised labour attempting to change the present industrial order, or when he opposed the extension of the franchise because it would mean giving votes to the discontented he was, in fact, breaking his own prohibition on the preaching of politics. And it is difficult to understand how the courts of the Church could make pronouncements in the political and economic field (albeit from an ethical standpoint) without ministers of the Church contributing to the framing of these pronouncements. It is almost as if Clow imagined the courts of the Church having an existence independent of those who sat in them.

Clow shares the view expressed by Flint in *Christ's Kingdom upon Earth* that whenever men regard the Church and the Kingdom as one, they lead themselves and others astray, but Clow means something very different from Flint. Other organisations such as the family and the city, the university and the state can and should contribute to the coming of the Kingdom. Clow made it clear, however, that within these organisations, only individuals who demonstrated faith in Christ and obedience to God could contribute towards the Kingdom. This does seem to raise the question of whether it was meaningful for Clow to say that the Church and the Kingdom are not identical, if, in fact, he allowed only those in other organisations and institutions who were Christians to make a contribution towards the Kingdom. It is certainly a very different view of the role that secular organisations can play in working for the Kingdom of God from that held by Flint. Flint believed that secular agencies contributed towards the Kingdom of God without these agencies being staffed by Christians.

Clow admitted that there were difficulties in uncovering Jesus' social ideals. He said that Jesus was not a systematic thinker, nor aware of modern conditions, nor a social reformer. He was sure, however, that Jesus taught that the basis of the Kingdom of God was 'an inviolable individualism'. Clow deduced that the Hebrew social ideal was 'that life can be lived rightly only on the basis of an inviolable individualism. That basis Christ accepted and enforced. Nothing is more certain than his jealous regard for and impassioned interest in the individual.' Clow believed both theologically and practically that the Kingdom of God could only be realised through individual Christian hearts and lives.

> Some are eager to try any method which promises to remedy some of the glaring wrongs of the time. Others are angry with the rich and their ways. Others are envious of their soft lives and dainty luxuries. Others are filled with a keen pity for the poor and their dark and narrow homes, and are moved by a desire to advance Christ's Kingdom by amending that social order which so grievously hinders it. They are like people who suffer from an obscure disease, and run off to any fair-spoken vendor, who proclaims his drug as a peculiar remedy.[10]

Clow insisted that Jesus envisaged a spiritualised Kingdom of God. It does Jesus a grave injustice to claim that he posed as a social reformer, and to ignore the mass and weight of his teaching which, according to Clow, make clear that he did not. What Jesus did was to plant the seed within men's hearts of a new social order. Clow, however, is quite clear about what did not interest Jesus about the new social order he envisaged. Jesus was not interested in the distribution of wealth. He never confused justice with equality. Neither poverty nor riches played a large part in his teaching. He dismissed earthly goals as things the Gentiles sought that had no place in the advancement of the Kingdom of God. He refused to deal with the issue of capital and labour in any form in which it was presented to him. He condemned covetousness in rich and poor, but he did not condemn wealth. Dealing with the tendency of Luke's Gospel to record Jesus passing severe judgements on the rich and expressing a favourable attitude to the poor, Clow preferred Matthew's spiritualising of the saying, believing that Luke misinterpreted Jesus by thinking he referred to material poverty whereas Matthew correctly realised that Jesus meant poverty of spirit. On the other hand, according to Clow, 'Jesus regarded riches, when honestly and honourably gained, as an *achievement*'. Jesus would not have approved of an attack on wealth:

That is neither just ethics nor wise economics. He would not sanction a law which would rob the individual of his liberty, even although it be a liberty to suffer, unless and until that liberty becomes a menace to the well-being of others. He would not distribute, as he did not distribute, frequent or easy or indiscriminate charity. He would endeavour to bring both the richer and the poorer, the employer and the employee into a new relationship to God and to each other. He would say both to capital and to labour, to rich and to poor, to master and to servant, to the man of many talents and the man of few, as to the man and the woman – 'What God hath joined together, let not man put asunder.'[11]

Jesus, Clow said, would not abolish capitalism because there is no reason to imagine that Jesus believed in economic equality, and his parables and his dealings with people of wealth show that he realised that the capitalist is essential. He derived from the parables of the pounds and the talents, of the labourers in the vineyard and the unmerciful servant his belief that Jesus laid obligations on the capitalist: honest and honourable service, generous oversight of labour and self-sacrifice on the occasion of need.

Because of his view of the teaching of Jesus about the Kingdom of God's relationship to social problems and issues, Clow would not allow the Gospel to be used in the cause of social improvement. The argument that environmental conditions influence spiritual commitment is not one that Clow accepted. 'Every man who knows the poor can recount numberless cases of homes, as holy as the home of Nazareth, maintained on less than £1 a week.' The view that very low income provides a disincentive to spiritual growth and development was one that was regularly used as an argument for the Church's involvement in the improvement of social conditions, and indeed was the conviction that led the Presbytery of Glasgow into the examination of housing conditions. Clow was someone who was inclined to state his case in terms of debating points, and this may be an example. Although he dismissed those who thought that faith cannot thrive in poor conditions on the basis that everyone knew of holy homes surviving on less than £1 a week, he stated categorically that

> the man who has not a living wage is prevented from entering Christ's Kingdom, or attaining that character which Christ declares to be the supreme achievement in life. If a man has not a decent living wage, he is deprived of the conditions of a healthful and moral life.

He immediately went on to state, however, that in his view a 'living wage' was not the same as the minimum wage being demanded by many Labour politicians and trades unionists. Despite his tacit acknowledgement of the effect of social conditions on spiritual attitudes, Clow's opposition to the

Kingdom of God being achieved through a social gospel is absolute because 'the only environment which is detrimental to faith and to purity is the environment of moral evil, not of industrial hardship'.

In the context of his individualist social theology, Clow said that the role and function of the Church was to be 'the special agency designed to bring in the Kingdom of God', so it is not surprising that the role he saw for the Church was 'to win men to Christ, to bring them into touch with God, to refine and perfect their character so as to make them citizens of the Kingdom'. Thus the Church's priority was 'not to make laws, not to lobby public questions, not to pronounce on the matter of hours and wages, not to play policemen in the streets, but to make men of faith'. Continuing his theme of the individual's responsibility for advancing the Kingdom, Clow said that the second duty of the Church was 'to expound the principles taught by Christ and to apply these principles to the lives of men'.

> Were every Christian man living in the world with eyes open both to good and evil, his conscience quickened to see the path of his own conscience, and his will strengthened to walk in it, the strife between capital and labour would not last for a week, and the revolt of woman, seeking a worldly sphere and a selfish economic independence, would die within every Christ-like heart.[12]

REVD ALEXANDER SCOTT MATHESON

Scott Matheson, who came into the United Free Church from the United Presbyterian tradition, was at the opposite extreme of the theological spectrum from James Denney and William Clow. His book *The Gospel and Modern Substitutes*[13] originated in a series of lectures he gave on Sunday evenings in September and October 1888 that were published the following year in the magazine *The Christian Socialist*. Matheson published two more substantial works, *The Church and Social Problems* and *The City of Man*.[14] *The City of Man* is a review of various social experiments, such as the Garden City (he was for a time a minister in England), and an argument for a considerable extension of municipalisation into such areas as school meals, inadequate parenting, the acquisition and development of land for housing, and improved sanitation. Matheson was a great admirer of the municipalisation that had taken place in Glasgow, where he was a minister before moving to Dumbarton. 'The Corporation of Glasgow,' he said, 'is now the Mecca of the municipal reformer.' Matheson's support for municipalisation was expressed against the background of his conviction that Christianity offered 'an ideal civic creed' which fashioned the ideal citizen, because Christ's preaching of the Kingdom of God was intended to have political implications.

The New Testament reveals the Kingdom of God as the Kingdom of Heaven upon earth, and the Sermon on the Mount is the manifesto of its Citizen-King. For every Christian the question comes to the front: 'Is the Sermon on the Mount a fantastic theory or a working programme of life?' To academic minds it seems a beautiful ideal hovering over our earth, of a kind with Plato's Republic, never realised and perhaps not meant to be realised. Christ meant his laws and relations of the Kingdom to be a guide for conduct, and he is no Christian who does not strive for their embodiment in every social sphere.[15]

Matheson said that when Jesus described his Kingdom as not of this world, he meant that the Kingdom's authority and principles did not derive from this world's understanding of power or from any human wisdom. He certainly did not mean that the Kingdom of God should avoid involvement with every aspect of life on earth. The emphasis on the end of time, which had been thought in the past to be a determining principle of the Kingdom of God, now required to be modified so that the emphasis was laid on justice, love and brotherhood here on earth. Matheson therefore applauded the theological shift from doctrinal to ethical issues. The chief strength of Jesus' teaching about the Kingdom of God, he believed, was its ethical content, but there had been a tendency in Britain to regard ethics as no more significant than pagan morality. The Kingdom of God envisaged progress not as 'individualistic but socialistic' and therefore the ethics of the Kingdom have to do with social cohesion rather than personal morality. This is summed up in the golden rule of doing to others what we would have them do to us, and so, crucially for Matheson, individualism becomes the consequence of the Kingdom's ethical stress on social justice, not the inspiration for it. So Matheson combined the individualism that is to be found in the Gospel (and therefore in the Kingdom of God) with the social involvement that he wanted to stress, and to which individuals affirmed within the community are further to promote:

> Justice includes the free play of individual character, the equal right of each to realise his nature and be what God meant him to be; it also includes that each man counts one, and nobody more than one; while it rises out of individualism into the great thought of the community, and sets forth fellowship, brotherhood and co-operation.

While Clow envisaged the primacy of individual salvation which then results in an individual's commitment to social justice and the promotion of social cohesion, Matheson saw the salvation of the individual emerging from the Kingdom of God. The Church must show that 'the Gospel of the Kingdom of God' contains not only the promise of individual salvation but likewise the 'clue to all social and economic difficulties'. Matheson concluded, therefore, that far from being a distraction from the real evangelical purpose of the Church, an involvement with social problems gives the Church an opportunity to commend the Gospel as being the power of God to social and personal salvation.

Matheson insisted that the Church's involvement with social problems, arising from the demands of the Kingdom of God, does not involve, as critics of political involvement have said, the substitution of material concerns for the true spiritual Gospel. The reverse is the case. A concern for social problems is an antidote to the commercialism and materialism of the day. The Church's duty, therefore, is to pursue social and ethical developments with vigour, to learn to support the best interests of humanity as they are taught through the social sciences, to preach the social gospel and to share with people the conviction that the Gospel is far broader than they have been told. Matheson believed, however, that the Church had not yet grasped the principles of social justice which, he said, were contained in the Gospel of the Kingdom of God, and so the Church had not yet understood the principles of a potentially reconstructed society which the Church had to teach.

Because there is a relationship between the duties of the individual as citizen and the Christian's commitment to the Kingdom of God, Church and state have mutual duties. The Church has a duty to train its members and the state to train its citizens to do justice to the principles they share and on which a stable and righteous society can be established. Therefore the whole machinery of the state should be devoted to supporting the Church's manifesto for the Kingdom of God, while the Church should set no limits to its influence.

> No limit should be set to the sphere of her action; no department of life should be passed by. Industry, home life, civic statesmanship, politics, the world of science and art, of literature and recreation – her gracious concept of the Kingdom of God should permeate and purify all. If the Church set herself to this task, backed by no authority but divine truth and constrained by no motive but divine love, her citizens could permanently lift the whole of public life from the quagmire of selfishness, secularity and animalism in which it is stuck, could make national religion a paramount fact, and change a nation of traders and seamen into a commonwealth of patriotic and Christian citizens.[16]

This vision of a return to a form of godly commonwealth is a firm feature of Matheson's social theology. It stems from his conviction that Church and state, Christian congregation and civic municipality are two sides of one reality which is ultimately theological; that the religious and the secular worlds owe to each other duties of mutual obligation because, in the final analysis, their aims are the same. So Christ's social ethic and the ideal civic creed are identical.

Because Matheson was such an admirer of municipal development and civic involvement, he embraced totally the Flintian doctrine that the Church must welcome and promote all secular movements and organisations that advance the Kingdom. It will be the duty of the Church to welcome such democratic institutions as village, municipal and county councils, and use them as fit organs for realising Christian ideals and carrying out such operations as the housing of the poor and temperance reform. Such powers are likely to be given to these councils, and when they come, the Church should have its members taught in the obligations of Christian citizenship and be ready to play a yeoman's part in the cause of social progress. From the pulpit men should be urged to volunteer for Christ's service in municipalities and village councils just as they are urged to come out for service in the Sunday School and Home Mission.

For Matheson, this understanding of the Kingdom of God had two important consequences. First, the Kingdom belongs to both men and women, who, he said, are equal, and this equality 'has been universally violated, almost entirely ignored'. There must be equality of opportunity, especially in education: 'Women should not be debarred from any educational advantage, from any sort of culture that is fitted to elicit, balance and complete their gifts of mind and heart.' In particular, Matheson believed that women had a particular place in the medical profession. However 'woman's Kingdom is the home; her highest office is that of wifehood and motherhood'. Second, Matheson believed that it had been the fault of English economists to concentrate on wealth creation rather than wealth distribution and that how best to redistribute wealth – which he insisted was the way to deal with poverty – was the primary task of the present generation of economists.

What Matheson said about the role of women and wealth distribution illustrates the dynamic he envisaged in pursuit of the Kingdom's principle of social justice. The principle of social justice is expressed through wealth distribution because it makes it more likely that individuals will achieve their potential. He asks,

> Why are 200,000 producers of wealth paid so small a proportion of the wealth they produce that they are obliged to rent one-room houses and live in surroundings that prevent decency, morality and health; that cause 82% of their children to die before they are five years old; and that abridge their lives to an average of twenty five years, as compared with an average of fifty years for the upper classes?[17]

The principle of equality of opportunity for women and men is a principle of the Kingdom of God precisely because it enables women to cultivate their potential and through achieving it make their own contribution to the commonweal.

Matheson's synthesis of the role of the individual and of society in social progress was an impressive one, and his knowledge of contemporary social experiments was wide. In two respects, however, he succumbed to a certain romanticism. He was a passionate supporter, for example, of the Garden City, and of the garden suburb, which, he said, enabled people to live ten or twenty miles away amid the beauties of the country and to come backward and forward to town for business. Matheson was similarly romantic about the 'model municipality' of Glasgow. The Glasgow of 1910, although clearly developing as a modern municipality, still displayed evidence of social deprivation and contained areas of great poverty, and the gap between these and the suburbs which he extolled was being widened by the very achievements he praised. Matheson does not appear fully to have realised this. The reason may lie in the other area of his thought where his romanticism is clear. The secular municipality he admired so much had, in Matheson's view, a theological goal, the city of God, the Kingdom of God. 'Any social order must stand in some veritable connection with the higher law of heaven. If it would be true and permanent it must recognise the presence and power of the living God.' And so Matheson's Kingdom of God turns out to bear a remarkable similarity to Thomas Chalmers' godly commonwealth, which the process of urbanisation had made it impossible for Chalmers to transfer from the rural economy of Kilmany to the urban situation in Glasgow. Despite Matheson's praise for it, municipalisation was not going to make the godly commonwealth any easier to achieve.

REVD DR DAVID WATSON

David Watson was minister of St Clements' in the East End of Glasgow and, for nearly thirty years, Vice Convener and then Convener of the Church of Scotland's Committee on Social Work, which expressed the Church's practical concern following the separation of responsibilities agreed with the United Free Church in 1909. He was instrumental in founding the Scottish Christian Social Union in 1901 and was its President from then until 1938. When the Church of Scotland Presbytery of Glasgow decided once more to investigate lodging houses and farmed-out houses, Watson personally visited both types of accommodation each night for a week, between 9.00 p.m. and 2.00 a.m., if not in disguise then certainly not recognisable as a minister. He was later to describe farmed-out houses as in many instances brothels. One of the results of Watson's visits was Glasgow Presbytery's Lodging House Mission, which had considerable success in providing meals and welfare services, and continues to do so. Watson helped organise the Church Congresses held at the beginning of the century and at which Robert Flint was often a keynote speaker. His practical involvement in social work stemmed from a developed social theology, which the Church of Scotland applauded but did not really embrace, and was expressed in three of the books he wrote.[18]

Two experiences fired Watson's social concern. When he was a student at the University of Glasgow, the Liberal MP John Bright was elected Rector. Watson was present at Bright's Rectorial Address, and in his autobiography he said he could never forget Bright's final sentence: 'I see before me men, women and children, hungry and ill-clothed, wan and wretched, passing on in never-ending and ghastly procession from the cradle to the grave.' Watson wrote that Bright's speech 'made him a housing reformer'.[19] The other experience that convinced Watson of the need for housing reform was the time he spent as a probationer minister in Paisley, in the congregation and parish where Robert Burns had served. 'It was while visiting from door to door in the poorer parts of the parish,' he wrote, 'that I came up against the housing problem and the slums of Paisley, which were terrible beyond anything I had seen in Glasgow.' He described what he had experienced in a series of unsigned articles for the *Paisley Gazette*.

Watson started from the conviction that the Church had not sufficiently preached about the Kingdom of God, and should don sackcloth in repentance, but he believed that the rediscovery of the Kingdom had been the greatest theological achievement of his day. The result of the Church's failure to preach about the Kingdom was its encouragement of social stratification, deference to wealth and rank, and neglect of social justice. The result of the rediscovery of the doctrine of the Kingdom was that the era of the Social Question began and the Church was committed to social transformation. Like Flint, Watson believed that the Kingdom of God will come on earth, and will involve a redeemed environment as well as redeemed individuals, and so the Kingdom is far wider than the Church because it will include nations and Churches. Like Flint he believed that the Kingdom will arrive through a process of evolution under divine control.

Watson's reliance on Flint is most clearly seen in what he said about secular agencies contributing to the advance of the Kingdom of God. He pointed out that science, by leading to improvements in health and sanitation, by providing labour-saving devices and inventing forms of transport, and by enabling industry better to create a society capable of redistributing wealth, 'provides the material framework for the Kingdom of God'. Watson went on to list contributions other than the overtly religious to the Kingdom of God in terms that were virtually a commentary on what Robert Flint said on the same subject. The contribution of literature has been its powerful portrayal of the ideal social state and its incisive criticism of those evil conditions that hinder the ideal. The contribution of philanthropy has been its strenuous and magnificent achievement in the sphere of practical helpfulness and social amelioration. The contribution of legislation lies in the many effective curbs it has placed upon human selfishness, cruelty and greed, and the many stimuli it has supplied to fair dealing and righteous conduct. The contribution of art has been its unwearied insistence on the eternal worth of beauty, and its everlasting appeal to the spirit of man. The contribution of commerce is the emphasis it lays on human solidarity, interdependence and mutual aid. The contribution of industry is its affirmation and demonstration of a truth that we forget at our peril, that upon work honestly and faithfully performed, and duty nobly done, must rest any true city or Kingdom of God.

The social nature of the Kingdom of God, according to Watson, stems from two of Jesus' institutions: the Lord's Supper and the Lord's Prayer. The Lord's Supper involved a divine society committed to love and service. 'We have by no means exhausted the full social import of the sacramental meal instituted by our Lord Jesus Christ. Watson maintained that just as the Lord's Supper made use of material things for spiritual ends, so the social gospel of Christianity required the Christian use of the material environment for people's spiritual development and well-being. The social aspects of the Lord's Prayer are implied in its constant use of plural pronouns. The initial emphasis is on the Fatherhood of God 'while the subsequent clauses emphasise social progress, social order, social duty and social worship'. Watson also derived his understanding of the social nature of the Kingdom of God from the Apostles' Creed, where the Fatherhood of God, the social expression of the faith at Pentecost and the Communion of Saints all point to it. The forgiveness of sins is the inspiration of the Church's ministry to 'the social derelicts and human wreckage of our complex and strenuous civilisation', while the doctrines of the resurrection, judgement and immortality imply that the present life is a preparation, and therefore 'everything which stunts character, handicaps life and hinders the free and harmonious development of personality should be removed'. Watson, however, criticised the creeds for being too 'metaphysical', with subtle theological definitions but no reference to the Kingdom of God or to social duty. He explained that the creeds were written to address issues that were disputed, but the unchallenged doctrines such as the Kingdom of God and its social implications are implicit in all the articles of the creed.

Watson expected that the Kingdom would be advanced through the work of committed Christians, but he went further and said that individuals mould Christian opinion and through the Church can transform society. *Social Problems and the Church's Duty*, published in the Church of Scotland's

Guild Library series, is a clear demand that the Church must consider and take a view on social and economic issues. Watson specifically advocates municipal housing, which he says should be funded by cheaper loans from the national government; he is critical of the unequal distribution of wealth and using unemployment as a tool of economic policy; he supports profit-sharing in industry; and all this because, Watson concludes, the Church should lead in social reform and social betterment for the advancement of the Kingdom of God.

Watson's social theology was open to the criticism that he placed insufficient emphasis on individual sinfulness. He wrote, for example:

> We have not sufficiently realised how largely moral evils spring from unchristian social conditions. We have too often been content to say that they spring from a depraved heart, without inquiring too minutely into the cause of human depravity. It might surprise some to learn that the devil or original sin had less to do with it than the slum and the public house.[20]

In wanting to provide a counterbalance to the tendency to blame poverty on individual fecklessness and irresponsibility, which was a view given considerable expression in evidence to the Housing Commission set up by the Church of Scotland Presbytery of Glasgow, it is understandable that Watson was tempted to underplay the role of human sin. When he gave evidence to the Royal Commission on Housing in Scotland, he was closely questioned about his view that social conditions effectively outweighed all other factors in their effect on the individual character. He was asked if he agreed that no matter what you do by personal influence, by every improvement in life that you can bring to bear, you are still faced with the results of overcrowding on the individual character. He replied, 'There is no doubt about that.' When he was asked whether his experience supported the view that family improvements would achieve nothing without better housing, he replied, 'Yes.' Watson was therefore led to a belief about the possibility of improving society that was perhaps optimistic. In evidence to the Royal Commission, he said that if there were better housing for the poor, supervised by caretakers,

> you would have very few of these destructive tenants. You would again educate, you would pull up these social laggards who as a class are the problem for us. The educative process would by and by result in eliminating or abolishing the class altogether.[21]

Watson's optimism about the effect of slum clearance was, however, tempered by a degree of realism:

> I should like to sound a note of warning with regard to the future. While

improving insanitary areas the authorities should keep a sharp look-out, and make sure that similar areas are not being allowed to spring up elsewhere, or the whole weary process of pulling down and clearing out will have to be gone over again.

Watson's understanding of the Kingdom of God as essentially pervasive meant that he had to rely on a number of assumptions which were to prove over-optimistic. He had to assume that the Kingdom's transforming power would bring about improved social conditions which, in turn, he assumed would produce regenerated lives. To be fair to him, at the time he was writing there had not yet been a sufficient amount of rehousing and improved housing for the discovery to have been made that these social improvements did not always result in the sort of reformed society that he envisaged. However, even given the political circumstances of Watson's day, one aspect of his attitude to the Church's involvement in the political arena is unrealistic. He believed that if great questions involving grave moral and social issues were disentangled from party politics, and placed separately before the country, for example by referendum, the Church might then intervene and throw the whole weight of its influence openly on the side of righteousness. He did not, however, make clear how moral and social issues could be separated from party politics if, as was so often the case, party divisions often reflected opposing attitudes on moral and social issues. G. R. Searle, surveying what he called 'the years of crisis' between 1908 and 1914, regarded the various movements that put pressure on the Liberal government – Irish Republicans and Irish Loyalists, syndicalists and suffragettes – as exhibiting 'a strain of moral absolutism'.[22] Far from it being possible to remove moral issues from the world of party politics, moral issues were invading that world at a time when the Church itself was divided on moral issues. The social, political and economic forces that 'pulverised' Britain in the early twentieth century had an effect on the Churches' social and political concern and commitment and also on the connection the Churches made between the Kingdom of God and developments in society. The moderate socialism of men like A. Scott Matheson was identified with much more radically socialist elements, and Matheson and others were marginalised. Middle-class support for the Kingdom of God on earth was likely to dissipate as moderate socialists became identified with what was perceived as dangerous radicalism. At the same time the growth of suburban housing changed the relationship between those who moved to the suburbs and urban society. Churches became a focus for people's leisure activity rather than for the promotion of the coming Kingdom of God.

NOTES

1. *The British Weekly*, 20 May 1909.
2. Denney, James (1910) *The Church and the Kingdom* (London: Hodder and Stoughton).
3. Ibid. pp. 101–2.
4. Gordon, James M. (2006) *James Denney, 1856–1917* (Milton Keynes: Paternoster Press).
5. Nicol, W. Robertson (1920) *Letters of Principal James Denney to W. Robertson Nicol, 1893–1917* (London: Hodder and Stoughton).
6. Ibid. p. 93.
7. Fleming, J. R. (1933) *A History of the Church in Scotland, 1843–1929*, vol. 2 (Edinburgh: T. & T. Clark), p. 228.
8. Clow, William (1913) *Christ in the Social Order* (London: Hodder and Stoughton).
9. Ibid. p. 91.
10. Ibid. pp. 142–3.
11. Ibid. pp. 261–2.
12. Matheson, A. Scott (1890) *The Gospel and Modern Substitutes* (Edinburgh: Oliphant, Anderson and Ferrier).
13. Matheson, A. Scott (1893) *The Church and Social Problems* (Edinburgh: Oliphant, Anderson and Ferrier); Matheson, A. Scott (1910) *The City of Man* (London: T. Fisher Unwin).
14. Matheson, *City of Man*, p. 13.
15. Matheson, *Church and Social Problems*, p. 19.
16. Matheson, *City of Man*, pp. 53–4.
17. Matheson, *Church and Social Problems*, p. 270.
18. Watson, David (1908) *Social Problems and the Church's Duty* (Edinburgh: R. & R. Clark); Watson, David (1911) *Social Advance: Its Meaning, Message and Goal* (London: Hodder and Stoughton); Watson, David (1919) *The Social Expression of Christianity* (London: Hodder and Stoughton).
19. Watson, David (1936) *Chords of Memory* (Edinburgh: William Blackwood & Sons), p. 66.
20. Watson, *Social Expression of Christianity*, p. 41.
21. *Report of the Royal Commission on the Housing of the Industrial People of Scotland, Rural and Urban*, Minutes of Evidence, vol. 1, 13 November 1913, p. 899ff.
22. Searle, G. R. (2004) *A New England: Peace and War, 1886–1918* (Oxford: Oxford University Press).

5

The House Divided Against Itself
The Kingdom of God in the Context of Debate

> Christ really meant his Kingdom to come on this earth, and all Kingdoms
> of this world, including the Kingdoms of trade, industry and politics, were
> to become a portion of his Kingdom
>
> J. Y. Simpson, 1908

The early sessions of the United Free Church General Assembly frequently
saw debates on the merits of candidates who were proposed for professor-
ships in the Church's three colleges in Aberdeen, Edinburgh and Glasgow.
What is surprising today is how often ministers who became well known for
their contribution to scholarship in one particular field had been proposed
for a chair in an entirely different subject. Professor A. M. Hunter, for
example, who became a widely acknowledged New Testament scholar, was
originally proposed in 1919 to the United Free Church Assembly for the
Chair of Church History in New College in Edinburgh, and some years
later for the Chair of Christian Ethics in Aberdeen. James Moffat, who
gained worldwide recognition as a scholar, interpreter and translator of the
New Testament into popular language, was Professor of Church History in
Glasgow for two years.

In 1911 the post of Professor of Christian Ethics and Practical Training
in Trinity College Glasgow came to be filled at the General Assembly. The
two front runners were William Clow, who, as we have seen, represented a
very conservative approach to social theology, and Robert Drummond,
minister of Lothian Road United Free Church, who said that all his life he
had a glorious battle to fight against conservative obscurantism. He was
Convener of the Church's Committees on Home Mission and Social
Questions, and in one Assembly said, 'We will feel that we are as truly
carrying on Home Mission when we are moving local authorities to remove
a slum as when we are preaching the need for cleansing of the heart and
renewing of the spirit.' As well as opposing Drummond's view of the
Kingdom of God, William Clow had attacked the direction taken by the
committees with which Drummond was involved, and so it is difficult to

avoid the conclusion that the vote was as much about the two different attitudes that had emerged within the United Free Church towards the Church's involvement in secular and social affairs as it was about the merits of two candidates for the Glasgow Chair. It is equally difficult not to regard Clow's success in the election as a considerable victory for those who supported his point of view.

THE GENERAL ASSEMBLIES 1904–7

It was because the United Free Church had already taken some tentative steps towards developing a social theology that the agreement reached in 1909 with the Church of Scotland had envisaged the United Free Church continuing its work in that direction. The report of the Life and Work Committee to the General Assembly of 1904[1] dismissed the fear many had, that cooperation with other agencies implied that the Church's answer to social issues was not unique. There was a real concern that if the Church was to support the state's growing involvement in social welfare, the role of the Church as the traditional provider of support for the poor would be eroded. If the Kingdom of God was defined in terms of meeting social need, the Church's role in advancing the Kingdom might become increasingly marginalised. The Life and Work report assured the Church that

> while we join with every movement, political, economic, social, which is fitted to improve the material condition of the poor by lessening their burden or increasing their comfort, we feel that the problem of poverty can only be solved by getting back to the moral foundations on which all human well-being can alone rest. Human conditions can only be equalised by heavenly consolations.[2]

The following year the Life and Work Committee was less proprietorial but still somewhat patronising:

> The Church recognises the authority of municipalities in their own sphere, and appreciates the value of their service to the common weal. Organised for the spiritual welfare of the people, the Church is free to welcome all light upon social problems, and improvements in social methods, by which obstacles may be removed, better conditions of living may be secured, prevailing evils may be lessened or removed, and her members may come, as for social so for spiritual ends, into helpful and sympathetic contact with the masses of the people.[3]

This report, however, firmly took the view that the Kingdom of God would be reached through individual effort and activity and that the role of the Church was to encourage the faith and commitment of Christian individuals as concerned and responsible citizens. But improved social conditions were insufficient. The Church must not stop at social work but bring to people the Gospel, 'which is still the only effective power for social regeneration'.

The underlying tension generated by the attempt to formulate social theology in the General Assembly was again clear in 1907. The Life and Work Committee referred to work done by what were called 'institutional churches' in the United States and in the north of England. These were congregations who made their church buildings available for the provision of recreational and leisure facilities, and educational and social opportunities for the underprivileged. David Watson's congregation in the East End of Glasgow and the Scottish Christian Social Union which he founded were to develop exactly this form of social mission, and of course today the practice is commonplace. The Life and Work Report of 1907 questioned whether the sort of direct involvement in providing resources to combat poverty had been fully considered but stated that it would probably be concluded that the Church's role and responsibility 'is more in the direction of inspiring its members to promote and support such agencies in their capacity as citizens'.[4] While recognising again that some took the view that involvement in social issues appeared to display a lack of confidence in the inherent power of the Gospel and salvation by grace alone, the Life and Work Committee rejected that view, claiming to have evidence from the work of institutional churches in the north of England that 'everything is done with the Kingdom of God in view'.

In the General Assembly of 1907 Mr (later Sir) David Paulin, who was for many years Vice Convener and then Convener of the Life and Work Committee, showed that he did not regard the Kingdom of God as requiring the Church's active participation in matters of social policy. So long as the Kingdom of God remained more of a rhetorical device than a theological reality in General Assembly reports and debates on them, then little progress would be made in providing a social theology for the Church.

> Anyone who has seen, as I have, the listening faces of hundreds of men, turned towards one as he speaks earnestly and simply of the things pertaining to the Kingdom must be satisfied that the movement towards it is one that should receive our unqualified and enthusiastic approval. We believe that by the guidance of the Spirit of God, our Church will in time arrive at a clearer comprehension of its duty in regard to methods of Christian work, which are full of interest, and which are fraught with great possibilities to the Kingdom of God.[5]

THE GENERAL ASSEMBLY OF 1908

Eight synods and presbyteries were not prepared to give the Life and Work Committee time to await the Spirit's guidance to accelerate the Church's involvement in social reform. They sent overtures to the Assembly, asking for a fresh look at how the Church fulfilled its social mission. The debate on these overtures took place against the background of a speech made in another debate earlier on the same day by William Clow, who attacked the fundamental principle of the Church's direct involvement in social issues. George Reith, who edited the Reports and Proceedings of the United Free Church General Assembly and also published his personal reminiscences of each of them from 1900 to 1929, described part of Clow's speech as 'in very poor taste' and Clow himself as 'a minister whose gifts and graces were honoured by all, but who had an unfortunate tendency to make tactless and ill-advised remarks'.[6] Clow had been chosen to second the adoption of the Home Mission Committee report, which had been proposed by Robert Drummond. Astonishingly for someone seconding a report, Clow said that he was opposed to the views that Drummond had expressed, and, he supposed, to many others who believed that the Church should deal with 'such questions as the housing of the poor, and the poverty of the home, and the squalor of the cities'. He said that the business of the Church was conversion and after conversion better social conditions would come:

> I, for one, fear lest this straining of men's minds towards the state of the body politic and the condition of labour and labour homes is not perilous and injurious to our one paramount duty – the proclaiming of the Gospel of Christ our Lord.

Clow went on to say that the Salvation Army, which had won a reputation for its concern for people's spiritual condition and not their physical welfare, had now 'fallen from that high ideal. They are now giving the strength which they once expended in bringing people to Christ, to establishing bureaux and labour homes, to colonising and to hotels and banks.' Clow commented sarcastically that a glance at the sermon titles in church advertisements in Saturday newspapers would show that those he described as 'weak men' were seeking popular approval by preaching about the housing question or the condition of the poor.

Towards the conclusion of his speech, Clow picked up on a comment that Robert Drummond had made in proposing the Home Mission report. Drummond had made a distinction between the Christian Church and the Christian people: the Christian Church's function is to make Christian people; the Christian people's function is to engage in the agencies and activities of the secular world. Clow responded vigorously:

What Christian people ought to do and can do, the Christian Church need not attempt. There are other societies divinely ordained to do these works of righteousness besides the Church. There is the Christian state, the Christian city, the Christian family. There are many other organisations and societies. I take a part so far as I can in all of these, but I am not going to call upon the Christian Church to take up the special work of the Christian state, the Christian city or the Christian family. Its own function is nobler and more imperative.

It is a measure of Clow's conservatism that he did not recognise the possibility of a systemic failure in the field of social welfare, and of his inability to read the signs of the times that he could speak of a 'Christian' state or city when in reality it was no longer possible to do so.[7]

A number of speakers during the Assembly distanced themselves from Clow's speech. One of them, Professor George Adam Smith, then of Trinity College Glasgow, said,

I am one of those who deprecate the opposition that some have sought in this Assembly to raise between evangelistic and social work ... It has been said that the Church should leave a very great deal to the Municipality and the State. I am one of those Church-workers who would leave just as much as possible of this kind of work to forces and individuals outside the Church. But when you have done that, when you have left all you can with a good conscience leave of social work, because individuals or institutions or societies outside are taking it up, there still remain in the experience of those who have been privileged to look into the needs of work in this direction – there still remain needs of social work who no-one else than the Church is fulfilling, and which therefore stand out as the Church's particular duty.[8]

Clow's speech to the 1908 General Assembly was important for a number of reasons. Those who wanted social and political engagement had seized the initiative by overturing the General Assembly. Clow's speech on the Home Mission Committee report, which preceded the debate on the overtures asking for a renewed examination of the Church's social mission, guaranteed that the debate on the overtures would not be a repeat of the earlier Assemblies' somewhat bland discussions but would be conducted in terms that revealed the wide gap between those responsible for bringing the overtures to the Assembly and people like William Clow. Second, Clow's speech became a rallying cry that those who agreed with him should be more vocal in expressing their deep reservations about the course of action on which the Church seemed to be set until then. And third, despite George Reith's comments about Clow, the speech gave Clow a prominence that until then he had not had, which was to be important in giving his opinions the greater importance of a college professor. Because of the election of professors in the United Free Church General Assembly and the fact that the colleges where they taught were under the direct control of the Church, the link between theologians and the Church was far closer in the United Free Church than it necessarily was in the Church of Scotland.

When the moderate socialist Glasgow minister Colin Gibb presented the overtures to the Assembly, he spoke of the alienation of the masses from the Church, of the dehumanising effect of industrialisation and of the appeal to the working class of a form of socialism that was opposed to religion. He wanted the Church to express concern not simply for the victims of poverty but about its causes. The Church had to show the working masses that it was their friend. Apart from the very small minority who opposed the overtures' proposal, the speeches that followed were of two sorts. Those who enthusiastically supported the overture saw the move as an important one for the Church to take in advancing the Kingdom of God. Others, however, were suspicious that the supporters of the Church's right to comment on and become involved with social policy had been working to achieve this surreptitiously. It is possible that in presenting the overtures, Gibb gave evidence that these suspicions might have some foundation. He said of the Secretary of the Life and Work Committee, and later of the Special Committee on Social Work, John D. Robertson of Leith, that two years earlier he had 'led the Church almost unknown to itself, upon these lines of enquiry and if the text of the Report of the Life and Work Committee, for which he was solely responsible [had] been in their hands, the overtures would have been differently framed'. By saying 'unknown to itself' Gibb was indicating that the significance of the step the United Free Church took in response to the overtures in 1908 was already foreseen in the previous Life and Work reports that Robertson inspired.

A future moderator, Dr Thomas Whitelaw of Kilmarnock, supported the overtures. He agreed with Clow that the solution to social problems ultimately lay with the state and that the Church's primary function was to preach the Gospel, but, he said, the Church could do a great deal to establish the Kingdom of God on earth by showing that the principles of the Gospel were relevant and could be applied to the improving of social conditions and the betterment of society. Scott Matheson urged the Assembly to formulate a social policy and thus attempt to apply the justice of the Kingdom of God to the social and industrial sphere. And Professor J. Y. Simpson, who specifically wanted a Department of Church and Labour to be set up, drew attention to the two views there were among those who were concerned about social conditions, one that demanded a change in the social environment, the other that depended on a change in individuals. Simpson stated that both changes were required because Christ really meant his Kingdom to come on earth, and, echoing Flint, went on to say that the kingdoms of trade, industry and politics, and those who belonged to them were to become part of Christ's Kingdom. The remaining speeches give the impression of being rather lukewarm. As Dr James Wells of Pollokshields put it, there was nothing in what it was being proposed to do with the overtures to which anyone might object. The Assembly decided to refer consideration of the overtures to its Life and Work Committee, to which twelve members who were signatories to the overtures were to be added.[9] Donald Smith's view was that this was a notable step[10] but it is far from clear that either the debate or the mood of the Assembly can be taken as an indication of growing support for a rigorous social theology. In his reflection on the debate, George Reith's judgement was that many members of the Assembly

> felt that though the projects of social service were excellent in their way, and appealed to some of the best instincts of good men, there was a real danger that the primary function of the Church to press the Gospel on the individual conscience would tend to become of secondary importance. To get at the mass through the individual rather than seek the individual through the mass seemed to them to be supremely the method of Christ, which his disciples were bound to follow. The above remarks are not so much matter drawn from Assembly speeches as reflections of talk amongst the members afterwards in the freer environment of intercourse in the corridors and the smoking-room.[11]

Although Reith's own attitude was clearly very similar to William Clow's, he was a shrewd commentator on the General Assemblies. It seems unlikely that, as Donald Smith suggests, he would have invented a mood, critical of the developing attitude towards social questions, if he had not sensed it himself. Crucially Reith prefaces his remarks about the new note which he heard being sounded at the 1908 Assembly by saying that the call for social service to be regarded as almost a necessary preliminary to the Gospel 'was not as yet very clear but it became clearer in subsequent Assemblies'. It was Clow's alerting of the Assembly to this new note, and the groundswell of support for him which Reith picked up in the corridors and the smoking-room, that justifies the conclusion that the 1908 Assembly's decision was a good deal less than a ringing endorsement of a commitment to social reform.

By the end of the 1908 General Assembly the lines of conflict had been drawn. It is clear that both sides had accepted without question two of Robert Flint's fundamental convictions, though in the United Free Church they tended to be attributed to A. B. Bruce, whose teaching on the Kingdom owed a great deal to Flint's work on the parables: first, that the Church and the Kingdom of God were not one and the same, and that the Church's role was to work towards the Kingdom; and second that other agencies, municipal, secular, social and political, all had contributions to make towards that Kingdom of God. The issue that divided the United Free Church was whether the Church's role was to lend support to measures of social reform, to contribute itself to the palliative measures required to ease the extremes of poverty or homelessness, or to create the sort of Christians who would carry the social implications of the Gospel into both the council chamber and the slums.

THE ECLIPSE OF SOCIAL CRITICISM

The 1909 General Assembly met against the background of the huge expansion of social welfare legislation undertaken by the Liberal government since 1906, and in particular Lloyd George's People's Budget which he had outlined a month or so previously. The Liberal government's welfare programme started the year it was elected when it permitted local authorities to increase rates in order to subsidise school meals. The Old Age Pensions Act of 1908 was to provide a modest, non-contributory pension of five shillings a week for more than one million people over the age of seventy by 1911.

Those in the churches from the days of Patrick Brewster onwards who had been expressing concern for the old, the sick and the unemployed were bound to regard these measures as of enormous importance. Those who saw the alleviation of poverty and the improvement of social conditions as steps towards the establishment of the Kingdom of God on earth will have regarded the government's social welfare legislation as the sort of 'good laws' which Robert Flint had argued contributed towards the Kingdom's advance. Those, like Scott Matheson, who believed that a redistribution of wealth within the nation was an essential step towards the Kingdom will have welcomed the element of redistribution in Lloyd George's People's Budget, which both increased the standard rate of income tax and imposed a tax of six pence in every £1 of income above £3,000 on those whose total income exceeded £5,000. And those, like Marshall Lang in the Church of Scotland and William Clow in the United Free Church, who represented a large body of opinion that traced social deprivation to excessive alcohol consumption, will have applauded the increased taxes on beer and spirits.

The report of the Life and Work Committee to the 1909 General Assembly attempted to provide a definitive and inclusive statement about the nature of the Kingdom of God. The Committee had been asked by the 1908 General Assembly 'to take into consideration in what ways the Church may best show her sympathy with, and lend assistance to, the various movements that aim at the betterment of society' and in particular to consider Professor J. Y. Simpson's proposal that a Department of Church and Labour be established. Clearly the Committee realised that its specific responses to these remits would depend on an answer to the question that the Assembly had never resolved: what the Church's role was in the establishment of the Kingdom of God. Various conferences had been arranged during the intervening year with secular agencies and socialist organisations in order to gather further the facts regarding poverty and industrial unrest, and a series of sub-committees had been appointed to look into specific subjects such as whether economics and sociology should be introduced into the training for the ministry, the propriety of establishing a Department of Church and Labour, and the problem of unemployment and the consequences of farmed-out houses. The first sub-committee was given the task of outlining Jesus' social teaching, which, it was recognised at the outset, was contained in Jesus' proclamation of the Kingdom of God. The Committee therefore proceeded to outline what it understood Jesus to have meant by the Kingdom of God. This was the moment at which James Denney chose to launch his attack on any understanding of the Kingdom of God that involved the active engagement of the Church with the political world. His timing was clearly a deliberate attempt to influence the General Assembly's attitude to the Life and Work Committee's understanding of the Kingdom of God and the Church's role in its advance.

It is clear from the language used throughout the report to the General Assembly that the prevailing view in the sub-committee, and certainly the one endorsed by the main Life and Work Committee in its report to the 1909 General Assembly, was a view of the Kingdom that would not have caused much anxiety to William Clow. At the outset the Kingdom is described as

> a spiritual reality. It is a society composed of children of one Father. This experience of sonship is Christ's first requirement. All his social aims and hopes are based on his demand for this personal, spiritual regeneration. And the preaching of the Kingdom is therefore the proclamation of the power of God's grace to deal with the needs of the world.[12]

To balance the individualism of this initial statement, the report then goes on to say that the Kingdom of God is also a social ideal. In rhetorical language somewhat reminiscent of the bland references to the Kingdom in the early debates in the United Free Church Assembly on social reform, the Kingdom is described as 'a brotherhood, a society of men and women living simple, happy free lives, serving one another in love. It is a regenerated social system.' There is little attention paid to the idea that the application of the values of the Kingdom might be considered appropriate in the contemporary area of social mission. The social gospel is described as what Jesus predicted would be the consummation of his Kingdom. The statement goes on to say that Jesus intended the social ideal of his Kingdom to be realised gradually through his disciples, and by his Spirit working through them. The aim of the Kingdom is eventual social regeneration as well as spiritual renewal.

Despite this, Donald Smith described the statement as clearly displaying the influence of the new social and theological liberalism, largely because it goes on to infer from the initial description of the Kingdom of God that there are

> elements in the present economic system which make the life Christ calls men to live hardly possible – such as unduly low wages, sweating of labour and oppressive conditions of work ... Extreme inequalities of wealth and poverty ... can hardly be said to reflect the mind of Christ [and] so far as modern conditions foster the alienation of industrial and other classes from one another, the whole spirit of Christ's words is against these conditions.

That clearly reflects the view of the twelve supporters of the 1908 overtures who were added to the membership of the Life and Work Committee. But the statement as a whole was much more of a compromise with the conservative element in the Assembly than Smith's judgement implies. It is true that the statement contained criticism of the present social system, but the United Free Church Assembly, as well as the Church of Scotland Assembly, had previously criticised low wages, sweated labour, poor working conditions, and extremes of wealth and poverty. The significantly conservative element in the statement was that it envisaged the eventual reform of these elements through the action of individuals. Social regeneration was to be achieved by Christ's disciples, and the Church's role was primarily to make disciples. In the references to the Kingdom of God as a spiritual and a social ideal, the statement is theologically specific in relation to the spiritual ideal. Everything depends on personal, spiritual regeneration. This contrasts with the vague, idyllic language in which the Kingdom as a social ideal is expressed – 'a society of men and women living simple, happy, free lives'. While there is indeed criticism of the existing social system, it is notable that in the specific references to the Kingdom of God there is no mention of a commitment to social justice in the present, nor to the alleviation of social distress or the reforms of social structures, which speakers in Assembly debates had described as integral to the Church's role in the establishment of the Kingdom. The fact that there was hardly any debate on the Life and Work Committee's statement lends support to the view that it was less than challenging. The Convener of the Life and Work Committee, the Revd W. M. Falconer, in presenting the report that contained the statement, the Revd Carnegie Simpson in seconding it and the Secretary of the Committee the Revd J. D. Robertson all spoke about the nature of the Kingdom of God, but the few speeches that followed concentrated on the recommendation that a Department of Church and Labour be formed and on the move to have it either rejected or sent back for further consideration. The proposal for a Department of Church and Labour was rejected, though with the sop to the committee that it might consider some experimentation in the area.[13] The following year the proposal to establish a Department of Church and Labour was watered down to appointing a new Committee on Social Problems. Two Glasgow elders, however, Buyers Black, a prominent Tory, and John Stephen, the shipbuilder, tried to abort even that proposal. In what Reith described as 'an animated debate', they unsuccessfully attempted to persuade the Assembly to 'decline to authorise any committee to interfere in the name of the Church with Labour and economic problems, or with duties pertaining thereto, which properly devolved on individual citizens or on the State'.[14]

It was the report of the Home Mission Committee in 1908 that had provoked William Clow's attack on the Church's growing involvement in social issues as a departure from its primary task. The Secretary of that Home Mission Committee, Dr John Young, was the Moderator of the 1910 General Assembly and he devoted almost the whole of a substantial opening address to the Assembly of that year to the subject of the Church's social concern in the context of the Kingdom of God. He said that the Church must attempt great things for the establishment of God's Kingdom because Jesus believed it was the primary aim in life. So 'what men talk of as the social problem is the religious problem of the day – primarily a problem for the Church'. Young basically still believed in the idea that the Church could be the most significant force in reforming society. He was determined to defend the view that the nature of the Kingdom of God required the Church to be involved in social issues. He said:

> the Church and nation have suffered much from the tacit assumption that the religious and the secular life can be lived in separate compartments, that religion may be kept apart from business transactions, from social relations, from civic duties and from political opinions … The Church of Christ has been too content to assume that large departments in private and public life are outside its sphere of influence, and has failed to declare the whole counsel of God as revealed, in its bearing upon social and civic relations, upon trade and industry, upon the economics and politics which rule the lives of men and of nations.

He vigorously defended politics as a Christian vocation and asked why 'they should be generally looked upon as "knavish tricks" except that they rhyme so in the national anthem?'

Young's speech, however, was a very carefully crafted one. For every reference to the Kingdom of God as involving engagement with the secular or political world, there was a balancing passage, making clear the limits Young saw to that involvement. However critical the Church needed to be of 'social theories and political nostrums', it could not but be sympathetic to the pleas for justice they contained. Young insisted that the headship of Christ involved his rule in every aspect of life, including business and civic life, but the Church had to 'teach men to face their duties rather than clamour for their rights; to care more for the excellence of workmanship than for the standard of wages'. The record indicates that this remark was greeted with applause. Young said at one point that 'the Church has to do primarily with the individual, and to aim at the change of heart which brings him into a right relation with God', but he added immediately that the Church cannot be indifferent to the sort of housing or the social conditions in which the individual has to live. A little later in his speech the balance was struck the other way round:

> There is no more serious hindrance to the progress of the Church and to the prosperity of the nation than the apathy of Christian men and women in regard to social wrongs. The Church has a duty to discharge in guiding public opinion and stimulating action by civic authorities in regard to matters which affect prejudicially the religion and morals of the community.

Almost immediately, however, Young went on to claim that the Church may not be able to become actively involved in schemes of social improvement or areas of social reform because 'it must scrupulously avoid all entanglements with class prejudice or party spirit'. And yet, he continued, the Church

> must also stand free from all complicity, active or passive, with social, industrial or civic wrong, and it must not fail in a clear, out-spoken testimony to the teaching of the word of God in relation to every evil or injustice which hinders the establishment of his Kingdom on earth.

It is when Young turned to discuss how the Church related to society that he made clear where he stood. In matters involving the Kingdom of God, the courts of the Church could only make representations on matters upon which there was a large measure of common agreement. The Church had scrupulously to avoid even the appearance of trespassing beyond its own province, just as it jealously guarded its own province against interference with its rights.

> There are not wanting in our day strong temptations placed before the Church, and conspicuous instances of their being yielded to, by which the Church may be secularised to a larger extent than the state or community is regenerated, and there may take place a socialisation or nationalisation of

religion, at the expense of religion ceasing to be a vital and energising force in the national life. Like its Master, the Church must refuse to act as judge and divider in matters that fall to be judged in other courts, to be entangled in affairs of state, or municipal politics which do not touch conscience or the liberties of Christ's House, or to be exploited by interested parties for secular ends and worldly schemes.[15]

The reported answer of Jesus when he was asked to adjudicate in a disputed inheritance, 'Who made me a judge or a divider over you?', was a favourite text of those who wanted to limit the Church's engagement in secular affairs.

Despite the vigorous attempt to be balanced, Young's speech to the General Assembly cannot be seen as other than an endorsement of the view that the Church's role was to inspire individuals with the Christian motivation to social reform, not to question the structural causes of social problems or to be involved as an institution in their solution. His attempt to achieve a balance at a time when the Church's attitude to social questions was potentially divisive is understandable. But ultimately this balance meant that Young's insistence that the Kingdom of God required a concern for social justice became little more than rhetoric when he envisaged the Church's engagement with society being limited and circumscribed by the need, for example, to comment only where there was widespread agreement, and his refusal to countenance any trespass beyond its own province. Perhaps Young was unable to recognise that the limitations he placed on the Church's actions effectively undermined the claims he made for its engagement with the secular world for the sake of the Kingdom of God. Perhaps he was employing a strategy, not unknown in the world of ecclesiastical politics, of adopting the language of radicalism while emptying it of all real content.

The General Assembly of 1911 continued to display the same degree of tension about the Church's role in social affairs. Young's successor as Moderator of the United Free Church Assembly in 1911 was the Glasgow Pollokshields minister, Dr James Wells, who came from the Free Church side of the United Church. Wells had been an assistant in the Wynds and then minister there between 1862 and 1867, and in 1867 became minister of the Barony Free Church. So, as he told the Assembly in his moderatorial address, he had spent a lifetime studying at close quarters the burning social issues of the day. He said the Assembly should be grateful to those who had brought about a new era where 'the housing of the poor, the pathetic child-life among them, their hardships from uncertainty of unemployment and insufficient earnings, their anxieties about the future, their distresses in sickness and old age ... are profoundly influencing the legislation of our day'. But he was insistent that the best hope for society lay in a religious revival and that the tendency to 'secularise' the Church in the interests of the poor had to be resisted. He said that the physical conditions of the poor depended on their moral conditions, which in turn reflected their spiritual condition. He saw little place for prophetic social preaching:

> Christ never directly intervened in the political or economic questions of his age. He refused to be a judge and divider between claimants for earthly goods, and he warned against covetousness. At the same time, he and his apostles enforced the civic duties. It therefore becomes the preacher to expound the social implications of Christianity. These themes, however, are soon exhausted, and the frequent handling of them sometimes wearies those who are in complete sympathy with the preacher.[16]

It may seem strange today to pay such attention to the addresses given by the Moderators of the General Assembly, given the lack of attention paid in the press to the whole business dealt with by the contemporary Church of Scotland General Assembly. In two ways, however, the moderatorial addresses of this period were ways by which a far wider audience than the General Assembly was addressed. The press provided very full reports including verbatim quotations of what moderators had said, and transcriptions of the moderator's address headed the copies of the proceedings and debates of the General Assembly which were sent to every congregation and widely read.

In presenting the report of the Special Committee on Social Problems at the 1911 General Assembly, Robert Drummond spoke about the importance of the Kingdom of God in the exploration of social theology. He also drew attention to the clear tension he sensed between his Committee and the wider Church: 'Is the Church sure that she has a social mission? This Committee stands for the recognition of it, but the whole movement of which it is a part is often spoken of with suspicion.'

The suspicion that Drummond sensed is apparent in the support that the Glasgow elder Buyers Black found for his opposition to virtually the entire content of the Special Committee's report. The Special Committee's proposal that the government should be asked to create a tribunal to arbitrate in industrial disputes was defeated, as was its request that the Assembly 'welcome' a series of booklets it had commissioned on social issues, including one written by Robert Drummond. A proposal to hold a Labour week in Glasgow was amended to require the prior permission of the Presbytery of Glasgow, and it was decided that the cost of the Labour week should not be met from central funds but would have to be raised by the Committee itself.[17]

The attempt by the Special Committee on Social Problems in 1911 to confront the Church with issues raised by industrial and social conditions through providing literature on a range of issues had been a rather minimal attempt to create interest in social theology. It was to be the last concerted effort on the part of those such as Robert Drummond who wanted to see the Church engage seriously with social and economic issues. Within a relatively short period of time, the Committee on Social Problems was recognised as little more than a token gesture in the direction of social criticism. A later Convener even described its report one year as platitudinous. Colin Gibb was soon to leave the parochial ministry; James Barr, who had always supported the engagement of the Church in politics, found parliament a more appropriate place to pursue social reform; and the views of James Denney and William Clow were only occasionally challenged.

In 1912, the Liberal government appointed a Royal Commission to investigate the housing of the industrial population of Scotland. Two prominent members of the United Free Church, the theologian and land-owner George Freeland Barbour and James Barr, then minister of St Mary's United Free Church in Govan, who later took over the chair, were both members of the Commission, to which John Robertson gave evidence – as, by then, Convener of the Life and Work Committee and Secretary of the Social Problems Committee of the United Free Church.[18]

Robertson was questioned at the start of his evidence about the view of the United Free Church that small and overcrowded houses produce indecency and immorality, and he was also examined by members of the Commission (one of them Freeland Barbour) who clearly did not think that the connection had been sufficiently established. Robertson gave evidence concerning the extortionate profits alleged to be made through farmed-out housing, which, he said, contributed to the spread of immorality, as nightly letting encouraged prostitution. He was again closely questioned about what he would do with those who could only afford to rent a room on a nightly basis and what accommodation there was for them. Robertson gave as his personal opinion that he was opposed to the letting of single-roomed houses except to single people or couples without children, that every house with two rooms or more should have a toilet and that there should be a wash-house for every four or five families. When asked how, if the Commission did decide that there should be a minimum standard of accommodation such as Robertson suggested, those on low wages could afford it, Robertson's answer was to propose a state-enforced minimum wage. (William Clow's *Christ in the Social Order*, published at the same time as Robertson was giving this evidence, may be regarded as his rejoinder to such a suggestion being made in the name of the United Free Church.) In fact the Commission took the view that rather than raise wages compulsorily, the State should, for a period of at least fourteen years, and working through municipalities, provide housing at affordable rent, though there was a minority report from four members of the Commission, including Freeland Barbour, who took the view that the local authorities could not bear the cost of housing alone and recommended that the state would have to provide subsidies for private enterprise to build houses at affordable but uneconomic rents. The evidence that Robertson gave went far beyond anything the United Free Church General Assembly would have been likely to support.

S. J. Brown sees the political divisions following the ending of the war in 1918 as significant in persuading leaders of the Church of Scotland and the United Free Church to silence the Church's call for a new social order. As we have seen, there is evidence that the commitment to social criticism and reform was unravelling in the United Free Church of Scotland from 1908, though the Church of Scotland appears to have been relatively unaffected by the tensions that beset the United Free Church. There are a number of reasons for this. First, the agreement to divide broadly the responsibilities of the two Churches, leaving social criticism to the United Free Church and social welfare to the Church of Scotland, meant that there were far more opportunities for strong differences of opinion to appear in debates in the United Free Church Assembly than in that of the Church of Scotland. Second, the Church of Scotland, which broadly identified itself with the Conservative Party, was less likely to include people who wanted to respond positively and enthusiastically to the reforming measures of the 1906 Liberal government than was the United Free Church. Third, the United Free Church contained both Conservative and Liberal elements in uneasy coalition. Its ministry included men like the conservative William Clow and the moderate socialist Alexander Scott Matheson, and thus in the United Free Church General Assembly debates on social issues, division over the Liberal government's social reforms was unavoidable. Fourth, there was an assumption within the Church of Scotland that as an established church, it was part of a partnership with civic, industrial and political institutions. Established church ministers were able to make effortless assumptions about their role in civic society, whereas William Clow, James Denney and Scott Matheson represented a nonconformist Church which, though confident in itself, was still struggling to identify what its role ought to be within Scottish society. Fifth, in the tumultuous years between 1910 and the out-break of war it became increasingly clear that social improvements were not producing stable conditions. The dramatic and extensive intrusion of the state into social welfare did not prevent a number of serious social and political crises that shook the entire edifice of the United Kingdom from about 1910 onwards. Social welfare as a route towards the Kingdom of God was, if not discredited, then at least tarnished. If the expansion of social welfare could not produce a stable and harmonious society it was unlikely to bring in the Kingdom of God. Most significantly of all, however, the United Free Church's energies, from 1909 onwards, became focused on the question of union with the Church of Scotland. And in that context the Kingdom of God took on an entirely new shape and function.

NOTES

1. 'Report on Church Life' (1904) *Reports to the General Assembly of the United Free Church of Scotland*, XVIII (Edinburgh: T. A. Constable).
2. Ibid.
3. Ibid. (1905).
4. Ibid. (1906).
5. Reith, George (ed.) (1907) *Proceedings and Debates of the United Free Church General Assembly* (Edinburgh: McNiven and Wallace), p. 188.
6. Reith, George (1933) *Reminiscences of the United Free Church General Assembly 1900–1929* (Edinburgh: Moray Press), p. 94.
7. Reith, George (ed.) (1908) *Proceedings and Debates of the United Free Church General Assembly* (Edinburgh: McNiven and Wallace), p. 260.
8. Ibid. p. 394.
9. Ibid. p. 264ff.
10. Smith, *Passive Obedience and Prophetic Protest*, p. 343 n.
11. Reith, *Reminiscences of the UF Church General Assembly*, p. 94.
12. 'Report on Church Life' (1909) Appendix, Section III 'Paper Prepared by Sub-Committee on the Social Teaching of our Lord', pp. 14–16.
13. Reith, George (ed.) (1909) *Proceedings and Debates of the United Free Church General Assembly* (Edinburgh: McNiven and Wallace), p. 250ff.
14. Reith, *Reminiscences of the United Free Church General Assembly*, pp. 114–15.
15. Reith, George (ed.) (1910) *Proceedings and Debates of the United Free Church General Assembly* (Edinburgh: McNiven and Wallace), p. 45ff.
16. Reith, George (ed.) (1911) *Proceedings and Debates of the United Free Church General Assembly* (Edinburgh: McNiven and Wallace), p. 44ff.
17. Ibid. p. 335.
18. *Report of the Royal Commission on the Housing of the Industrial Population of Scotland, Rural and Urban, Minutes of Evidence*, vol. 1, pp. 129–36, 14 March 1913.

6

Full Circle

Social Theology and Criticism in the Inter-War Years

> We have, as a divided Church, been impotent to deal with the broken
> fellowships in political society that brought our nation to the verge of
> disaster in Ireland, in the industrial sphere with the labour wars; in the
> community with its extremely rich and extremely poor; and in the great
> feminine movement. We have been out of touch with, and that despite our
> most earnest endeavours to reach, the large community of labour.[1]
>
> John White, sermon, 1917

In 1926, the Church of Scotland's General Assembly was invited to
congratulate the Scottish Christian Social Union on the twenty-fifth
anniversary of its founding by David Watson in 1901. Watson became
Chairman and was able to enlist Church leaders such as John Marshall
Lang, R. H. Story and George Adam Smith into the Union as well as others
who were known for their concern about social problems. The aims of the
Union were:

> To claim for the Christian law the ultimate authority to rule social practice;
> to affirm the social mission of the Church, and make practical suggestions
> as to how that mission may best be fulfilled; to investigate, where necessary
> the social and economic facts in different departments of the national life,
> and to study how to apply the truths and principles of Christianity to the
> problems arising therefrom; to take action, as occasion arises, for the
> furtherance of specific reforms.[2]

At the 1926 General Assembly, Dr John White, who had just completed his
year as Moderator and whom S. J. Brown describes as the person who 'more
than any other church leader defined the social ideal for Scottish
Presbyterianism' at the time,[3] spoke to the motion marking the Union's
semi-jubilee. He began somewhat ungraciously by congratulating the
Chairman and Executive 'on any service they may have rendered by laying
emphasis on the social mission of the Church'. He ended his speech with a

claim which those who belonged to the Union may have seriously questioned: 'No one who thinks clearly will admit that our present social and industrial system can truthfully be described as non-Christian.'[4]

David Watson and Professor William P. Paterson were the strongest advocates of a view of the Kingdom of God that envisaged it advancing as social conditions improved, where there was considerable redistribution of wealth and relations between capital and labour were thus transformed, and that saw the Church having a responsibility to engage actively with the social, political and economic processes by which society would be made more equal and just. It was a view of the Kingdom of God that was to disappear within the Church of Scotland for virtually a generation, ironically because of another cause of which Watson and Paterson were leading supporters, the movement for the reunion of the Church of Scotland and the United Free Church. S. J. Brown has commented that in the years leading up to the union of these two Churches in 1929 Church leaders so concentrated on the pragmatic politics of ecclesiastical union that they lost sight of the chief end of the Church: to witness to the coming Kingdom of God.[5] That is undoubtedly an accurate judgement, but these Church leaders would have found it a very puzzling one, believing as they did that the reason for pursuing reunion was precisely to advance the Kingdom of God, and that they had constantly pleaded the cause of the Kingdom in promoting the cause of reunion. From the first to the final draft of what became known as the Articles Declaratory of the Constitution of the Church of Scotland, which made the reunion of 1929 possible, the advancement of the Kingdom of God was claimed to be the purpose of the Church and the duty of the nation. The first, and unalterable, Article Declaratory commits the Church to labour 'for the advancement of the Kingdom of God throughout the world', and the sixth says that it is the duty of the nation 'to render homage to God, to acknowledge the Lord Jesus Christ to be King over the nations … and to promote in all appropriate ways the Kingdom of God'. As the movement towards reunion proceeded, however, the view of the Kingdom of God advancing as the Church became engaged with social, economic and political issues was considerably diluted.

THE THEME OF THE KINGDOM IN UNION DISCUSSIONS

A brief account of the reunion movement's early stages will be helpful in putting the use of language about Kingdom of God into the context of the union negotiations. At the third Church of Scotland Congress held in 1904, Dr Archibald Scott, a former Moderator and Convener of the General Assembly's Business Committee, suggested that the reunion of Presbyterianism would be in the interests of the Kingdom of God. In 1907 he persuaded the Presbytery of Edinburgh, which in turn persuaded the General Assembly, that there should be a conference of the Church of Scotland and the United Free Church

> so as to secure that the resources and gifts at the disposal of each of them would be utilised to the utmost in a collective, harmonious union and effect ministration to the spiritual and social necessities of the country and to the furtherance of the Kingdom of God more efficiently.

In November 1909 the first meeting of representatives of the two churches, one hundred from each, took place. As the committees met separately and in joint conference it became clear that if there were to be a union, the United Free Church would require to be satisfied that its principles, of the spiritual independence of the Church from the state and of the Church's reliance on the voluntary givings of its members, would not be compromised. On the other hand the Church of Scotland held very dear its historic claim to establishment and its entitlement to financial support from the endowments paid by the heritor landowners. It seemed as if the principles of the two Churches could not be resolved without conflict and that drawing an amicable conclusion to the conference might be preferable to futile argument.

The Church of Scotland's principal law adviser (Procurator), the advocate C. N. Johnston (later the judge Lord Sands), produced a memorandum that proposed a roadmap for union. Sands proposed that a new constitution for the Church of Scotland should be drawn up making clear both continuity with the national Church of the Reformation and insisting on freedom from any external control in doctrine or government. After this constitution had been agreed, parliament would be asked to pass an act acknowledging that it reflected the legal situation. A commission would then be appointed to deal with the question of the Church's endowments and the Church of Scotland would make no claim to exclusive privilege. The memorandum was unanimously approved by the General Assembly of 1912 and the United Free Church Assembly was virtually unanimous in giving its committee of one hundred authority to negotiate with the Church of Scotland on the basis of the memorandum.

By 1913 the terms of the memorandum were public and the Church of Scotland's committee began to produce draft Articles Declaratory. That winter considerable disquiet about the steps taken so far towards reunion was widely expressed. There was opposition to the statement of the Church's doctrine outlined in Article 1 both from a High Church group led by Professor James Cooper of Glasgow University and from more liberal churchmen who feared that the list of fundamental doctrines could stifle theological exploration. The powerful Clerk of the Presbytery of Glasgow, William S. Provand, publicly expressed concern that the Articles would be rushed through the Assembly and presbyteries without sufficient discussion. Other presbyteries

expressed misgivings about the contents of the memorandum and the draft
Articles, and Dr John White, who at the time was Secretary of the Church
of Scotland's committee conferring with the United Free Church, felt he had
to travel the country attempting to allay fears. In December 1913 he wrote
to the Moderator, Dr Wallace Williamson of St Giles' Cathedral, saying
how concerned he was about the opposition to the proposed roadmap for
union,[6] and Wallace Williamson confirmed that as he travelled he was also
encountering similar concerns that the United Free Church was forcing the
Church of Scotland to make unacceptable concessions. In 1914 White
persuaded the Assembly to seek informally the views of presbyteries on the
Articles Declaratory but meanwhile to authorise the resumption of
conference with the United Free Church. At this point the outbreak of war
caused formal discussions between the Churches to be put on hold. The
movement for reunion had been launched by Archibald Scott for the sake of
the advancement of the Kingdom of God, as Robert Flint envisaged it, and
it was supported by men such as John Marshall Lang and William P.
Paterson because they believed that a reunited Church would be the better
able to combat social, moral and religious problems. In 1914 the strongest
opponents within the Church of Scotland of the movement for reunion were
those who disagreed with Archibald Scott's conviction that considerations
of ecclesiastical status should be subordinated to the cause of the Kingdom
of God.

Talks about reunion resumed in 1919 against the background of post-
war tension and pessimism. National strikes in the mining and railway
industries were threatened. Unemployment was on the increase. A general
strike to secure a forty-hour week was called for in Glasgow, where within
a year, Labour candidates were to win eighteen of the thirty-seven seats in
the election to Glasgow Corporation. Professor W. P. Paterson was the
Moderator of the Church of Scotland's General Assembly in 1919, and when
he paid an official visit to the United Free Church Assembly on the day when
the two Churches were to be asked to resume discussions, he stressed that
in his view the two Churches 'struck the same note ... there was the same
religious message, the same realisation that the Kingdom of God included
individual salvation and social salvation, the same emphasis on the watch-
word of the supremacy of Christ in all spheres'.[7] In his moderatorial address
to the Church of Scotland Assembly, Paterson asserted his belief in Flint's
understanding of the Kingdom of God:

> In the modern period, marked by the social upheaval attendant on the
> Industrial Revolution and the progress of democracy, the Protestant Church
> tended to regard the realms of politics and business as lying outside the
> Kingdom of God and to be satisfied with exhorting industrial Christians to

keep their integrity and avoid the temptations of the world ... More recently there has been a revival of the older and worthier conception that the laws of God require to be positively applied in all spheres, including the political and economic.[8]

In the year he was Moderator, Paterson, along with David Watson, edited a book of essays on social evils and problems.[9] Though not a particularly well-known figure, more than anyone else he continued to speak and write about the Kingdom of God in terms almost identical to those of his teacher Robert Flint, whom he followed into the Chair of Divinity at Edinburgh. In his own contribution to *Social Evils and Problems* Paterson accepts without question that the Church's vocation is to work for the advancement of the Kingdom of God. While Jesus thought of the experience of the converted individual as the 'chief good' of the Kingdom of God,

> he also pointed to the goal of a perfected society, and the Church, which is his instrument, should include both in its vision. The Kingdom of God, it is also to be remembered, was expected by him, not merely to give rise to a Church, but to leaven the whole of human society.[10]

The use of the word 'merely' and the reference to the parable of the leaven echo perfectly the views of Robert Flint. Paterson regarded the family as ideally the Kingdom of God in miniature, 'subject to a rule judiciously compounded of justice and love, founded on a vow of faithfulness and purity, serving as the nursery of character, the school of virtue and piety, and the haven of happiness'.[11] In that context he regretted two moral evils he believed to have resulted from capitalism: the loss of the personal ties linking master and servant and the strife that tends to accompany differences in wealth. While he recognised that justice and humanity had become hallmarks of the political parties, he regretted that those in power tended to promote sectional interests. He was unwilling, however, to identify any economic or political system as permanently secure.

> The truth is that the industrial and social organisation with which we are familiar has been for a certain period the best practicable system for ensuring material progress and diffusing general comfort; but it was preceded by other systems which were better suited to the conditions of earlier times. So it may well be followed by another which will work as smoothly and beneficently under the changed conditions of the future.[12]

S. J. Brown sees support in Paterson's moderatorial address and *Social Evils and Problems* for his view that the Presbyterian Churches in Scotland

> committed themselves to work for the thorough reconstruction of Scottish

Society. Church leaders promised to work for a new Christian commonwealth, ending the social divisions and class hatred that had plagued pre-
war Scottish industrial society ... the Scottish people would be brought back
to the social teachings of Christianity and strive together to realise the
Kingdom of God.[13]

It is perfectly true that Church leaders and General Assembly deliverances
used language that justified that view. What is less clear, however, is that

> The post-war economic stagnation ... soon threw a shadow over the
> Churches' promises. In the face of continued social division, the Churches
> lost confidence in their social witness and withdrew from their pledges to
> work for social reconstruction.[14]

Post-war stagnation and industrial unrest did have a profound effect on the
Churches' view of society. But as we have already seen, before the First
World War broke out, the General Assembly of the United Free Church,
which through the agreement of 1909 had been given responsibility for
developing social criticism, had already rejected the view that the Churches
should be involved in working for social reconstruction as a contribution
towards the Kingdom of God. From 1919 to the reunion of the Churches in
1929 the language of the Kingdom of God was used constantly, but as we
shall see, it was an understanding of the Kingdom of God that was very far
from the view of Paterson and Watson. Because there had been very little
exploration of social criticism within the Church of Scotland, theirs had
been lonely voices, and with the post-war revival of the negotiations towards
reunion, their view of the importance of social reconstruction in the
advancement of the Kingdom of God was rapidly and deliberately eroded
in the context of economic and industrial problems by the man who became
the leading figure in Scottish Presbyterianism.

VERY REVD DR JOHN WHITE

It was during the 1919 General Assembly that the decision was taken to
create a Church and Nation Committee 'to watch over those developments
of the nation's life in which moral and spiritual considerations specially arise,
and consider what action the Church from time to time might be advised to
take to further the highest interests of the people'. Donald Smith regards
this as 'the most notable milestone of all ... in the gradual awakening of
social criticism in the Church of Scotland'.[15] That judgement is only possible
if the views of the Church and Nation Committee's first Convener, John
White, are ignored, for White held that any action the Church might be
advised to take was very limited in scope. He never ceased stressing that the

Church had no right, authority or knowledge to comment on detailed political or economic policy:

> Our Lord preached a Gospel of spiritual redemption not of social reform. The Gospels have nothing to teach us about the economic problems of distribution. Our Lord pointedly refused to act as an arbiter in a disputed question of ownership. The Church has only to do with the motives and desires and passions which lead to disputes about the distribution of wealth. We have no right to say that one system is more Christian than another.[16]

As White gradually became acknowledged as the leader of the movement for reunion, it was his minimalist view of what the Kingdom of God would amount to that became important in the atmosphere of reunion.

In 1920 the Church of Scotland General Assembly approved the Articles Declaratory, and in 1921, parliament passed the Church of Scotland Act, which confirmed that the Articles were legal. As we have seen, there are two references in the Articles to the Kingdom of God. It appears that on the road to reunion, the Kingdom of God was only given serious consideration on one occasion, in 1915, when there were informal conversations between leaders of the two Churches about the draft Articles. The Vice Convener of the United Free Church Committee, Dr John Young, feared that giving the state a duty to promote the Kingdom of God effectively granted it permission to do whatever it liked to promote what it regarded as in the interests of the Kingdom. He said that in his view there should be no reference at all to the Kingdom of God in the Articles. Explaining Young's objections in a letter to John White, the Convener of the United Free Church Committee, Dr Archibald Henderson, wrote that Young took this view because 'scholars and theologians are far from agreement as to what [the Kingdom of God] means; and certainly as used in the New Testament it has different significances in different connections'.[17] We have seen how the Kingdom of God was the context of serious disagreement within the United Free Church, and that when he was Moderator of its General Assembly in 1910 Young had struggled to maintain a balance in his address to the Assembly between the two strongly held views of it. Young's stance in 1915 signalled that the Kingdom of God might again become the focus of tension and disagreement, and the last thing John White would have wanted was for the support of the United Free Church to be undermined at precisely the time when there were serious challenges to the Articles Declaratory within the Church of Scotland.

John White's biographer rightly describes him as not a man to use pliant phrases that could be taken to mean this or that or something else. Throughout the 1920s, when White spoke to presbyteries up and down the country about reunion, he always said that its purpose was 'the great objective of the advancement of Christ's Kingdom at home and abroad'.

When White spoke about the Kingdom, however, it was a vision, an ideal, a goal, but he was reluctant to outline what the vision contained, or the ideal amounted to, or the goal encapsulated. He was very clear in his own mind that the advancement of the Kingdom of God must not lead the Church to involve itself in any criticism of social or economic policy. The question may be asked, however: if, as the Articles Declaratory stated, the nation had a duty to promote the Kingdom of God, how was the nation to be informed of what steps would promote the Kingdom, or indeed if it were failing in some way in its duty to promote the Kingdom, if the Church was forbidden to comment on political, economic and social affairs? Was that also to be left to the influence of lives regenerated through the Church's influence?

White was elected Moderator of the General Assembly of 1925, and in his moderatorial address he said:

> Let it be clearly understood that we are not called upon to elaborate any scheme of social economics or politics; but we are required to declare that the teachings of the Kingdom of God when applied to the problems of today, bring into prominence two governing principles of human value and human comradeship – the equal and infinite value of every personality in the sight of God, and the brotherhood of man … [The Church] will avoid darkening counsel by words without knowledge, and refrain from the technical side of economics, which is a science for experts, and in which the Church has no authority. It will, however, go into the midst of the contending forces, if possible between them, and seek to act as a mediator.[18]

Addressing the Lord High Commissioner at the close of the 1925 Assembly, White said that a united Church had to bring the Gospel of Christ, which was the solution of every problem of society, to bear on the whole of organised life. If, however, the only thing the Church could do to advance the Kingdom of God was to proclaim the infinite value of every individual in the sight of God and the brotherhood of man, then White was open to the charge that he had reduced the essence of the teaching of Jesus to a useful slogan. Flint's passionate argument in favour of cooperation between the Church and secular agencies, and the recognition of the contribution that the arts, science and literature made to the Kingdom of God, despite the invocation of the Kingdom in the Articles Declaratory, had been replaced by White's assertion that a united Church could alone contribute 'the chief share' to the moulding of the new life of the world.

Both the relevance and the effectiveness of White's social theology were tested in his moderatorial year. Just a few weeks after the Moderator had said to the General Assembly that 'social conditions were better and not worse' and that 'the poor were not poorer', Prime Minister Stanley Baldwin told the nation that 'all the workers of this country have got to take reductions in wages to help put industry on its feet'. The mine owners gave one month's notice of their intention to end the existing wages agreement and a strike was only prevented by the appointment of a Royal Commission, though the government began planning emergency measures as talk continued of a national strike. In March 1926, while it proposed future improvements in the mining industry, the Royal Commission also recommended an immediate reduction in wages. The mine owners demanded not only lower wages but longer hours. The miners responded with the slogan 'Not a penny off the pay, not a minute on the day'. At the beginning of May the miners were locked out, and the Trades Union Council called a general strike, which lasted nine days, with over a million and a half workers withdrawing their labour. In Glasgow, there was a very positive response to the strike call, but by the time it ended, 7,000 people, including 300 students, had been persuaded to break the strike and to volunteer to man the docks and maintain supplies of coal, food and milk. Before the General Assembly adjourned for two weeks to allow for the production of its papers, which had been hindered by the industrial action, the strike gave John White, as the retiring Moderator, an illustration of how much the Kingdom of God was needed. In the country as a whole, he said,

> when we turn from the bright vision of the Kingdom of God on earth, and look at society as it is today, on the prejudice, jealousy and sheer ignorance that sets class against class, the spirit that puts self-interest against the service of the community, does not the contrast summon us with a new insistence to give the Lord no rest, and to hold not our peace till he makes Jerusalem a praise on earth.[19]

But the bright vision of the Kingdom of God on earth again amounted to the dream of the recognition of every individual's worth and the brotherhood of man, with no suggestion as to how there might be any approximation to the dream in the contemporary situation. White proposed that the Church could be a mediator between mine owners and miners, but the mine owners refused to accept his offer, pointing out, not unreasonably, that White had consistently said that the Church lacked the competence to make economic or political judgements.

What mattered to White about the Kingdom of God was that it was a goal that transcended the divided Churches. He could appeal to the two Churches to overcome any reservations about union for the sake of the greater prize of the advancement of the Kingdom. He said in his 1925 moderatorial address, 'Our Presbyterian divisions indubitably weaken the Church's testimony and its authority as God's ordinance, and greatly hampered and counteracted its effort to advance his Kingdom.'[20] That same year the Moderator of the United Free Church General Assembly, its senior clerk Dr James Harvey, made exactly the same point when he said that competition between denominations 'weakens the Church of God and the extension of the Kingdom of God'. When John White asked the General Assembly of 1928 to approve the final Basis and Plan of Union and to seek the approval of presbyteries for it, the importance of reunion for the Kingdom of God emerged again. He said that the Church had been too self-centred on its own concerns.

> The Church is called to be what it was intended to be, the chief agency of establishing the Kingdom of God in our land. Its efficiency for this great task will be increased when, through reunion, there is brought about the liberation of the forces of Christian zeal and brotherhood and sacrifice which would banish the weakness, waste and littleness of conception which has so often marred religion in Scotland. When we consider the divisions of our Presbyterian Churches alongside such tremendously grave questions, we see how urgent was the need of some healing; and that nothing short of over-mastering necessity should keep separate those Churches which shared a common inheritance in the historic Presbyterianism of the country, and are one in all essentials of worship and doctrine.[21]

THE KINGDOM IN UNITED FREE CHURCH DISCUSSIONS

The discussion of reunion in the General Assembly of the United Free Church also focused on its importance for the Kingdom of God. There were a number of references to what Principal Rainy had said about the union in 1900 between the Free and United Presbyterian Churches: 'I trust in the end, though I do not know how it is to come, yet come I trust it will, a larger Presbyterianism for Scotland, devoted to the advance of our Lord's Kingdom.' In 1921 Dr Archibald Henderson described the union made possible by parliament's approval of the Articles Declaratory as one 'that would further the interests of Christ's Kingdom'.[22] Two years later, Sir Thomas Henderson MP, seconding the motion supporting further moves towards reunion, believed they 'would lead to ... a great advance in the establishment of the Kingdom of God in the world'.[23] And the following year, an elder, J. Forrester-Paton, hoped that without denominational distractions the Church might be a more effective instrument for the extension of the Kingdom of Christ,[24] although in 1926 he urged delay in approving the final stages of reunion 'so that they might go forward wholeheartedly and unitedly along whatever course would advance Christ's Kingdom in Scotland'.[25] In 1927 Principal Alexander Martin of New College, who had taken over the convenership of the United Free Church's negotiating committee, was able to report such remarkable progress that he could ask for general approval to be given to a draft uniting Act. He said he was able to see the time drawing near when 'as one undivided communion we will take counsel for the promoting of God's Kingdom in our own land and across the seas'.[26] The rhetoric of the Kingdom of God was perhaps being used to attempt to overcome the degree of apathy there was among the congregations of the United Free Church towards the union. It was also held out as a vision that could be appealed to as surpassing ecclesiastical differences, but whose advance did not have to be described, though the missionary Dr Donald Fraser did try to deal with its content when he was Moderator in 1922. He stressed that it was not the task of organised religion alone to bring in the Kingdom of God: 'It is the privilege of every force that is moving in the world, of government, commerce and industry, commerce and all colonists.'[27] Echoing the teaching of Robert Flint and A. B. Bruce, he told a story of a man who was asked what he did for the Kingdom of God and who replied, 'I bake,' and when he was asked to describe something religious he said, 'I bake.'[28] Donald Fraser's vision was of a Kingdom so engaged with business and commerce that others would say of their work for the Kingdom: 'I build decent homes.' 'I pay men worthy wages.' 'I give my employers an honest day's work.' 'I provide clean laughter and good music.'

There was more sympathy expressed by individuals in the United Free Church Assembly for the Church's responsibility to comment on and actively engage with social, political and economic policy than John White would have allowed. In 1919, Professor W. M. McGregor, in his moderatorial address, said:

> It is a better and more healthful sign of the health of our perceptions when we grow hot against our present system of housing and our present system of hours, and are even organising war against this present plague of poverty in which for ages men have acquiesced, as if it were of divine appointment.[29]

McGregor quoted Henry Scott Holland, whose Christian Social Union had inspired David Watson:

> The new labour movement sets in the foreground not the skilled artisan but the outcast unemployed, the broken, the unskilled, the casual. That may be economically disturbing but it is fully in character with His mind who does not break the bruised reed; and the fact that it can be noted as characteristic of the new temper is a symptom of a quickening hope.[30]

That year, the miners went on strike for an increase in wages, and there were dark threats of a general strike. The following year the economy crashed. Unemployment doubled, and never fell below 10 per cent. Principal Martin of New College was not only Moderator in the year of reunion but had previously been Moderator in 1920 and had then criticised the lack of support for those who had suffered the depersonalising effects of the Industrial Revolution – and, though conceding that the industrial unrest at the time was doubtless accompanied by gross selfishness, he sympathised with 'the worker who is, for the most part, a mere factor in a vast and complicated production process ... over which he has no control'. And he quoted with approval the remark of Oliver Cromwell that 'it is part of a man's religion to see that his country be well governed'.[31] In 1924, the Revd John Mansie, the Convener of the Social Problems Committee, insisted that housing conditions in the country were a barrier to the advance of the Kingdom of God,[32] and he was given support from the chair when the Moderator, Dr Alexander Insch, who ministered to a working-class parish in Dumbarton, said that there were housing conditions where it is 'well nigh impossible' to be a Christian. There were individual voices in the United Free Church attempting to address social, economic and political issues in the light of their understanding of the Gospel, but they tended not to link these to an understanding of the Kingdom of God which included social improvement, economic justice or political concerns.

THE TERRITORIAL PRINCIPLE

The third Article Declaratory stated that '[a]s a national church, representative of the Christian Faith of the Scottish people it acknowledges its distinctive call and duty to bring the ordinances of religion to the people in every parish of Scotland through a territorial ministry'. Every bit as much as the references in the Articles Declaratory to the Kingdom of God, the commitment in them to a territorial ministry was necessary if the union was to hold together both the High Church group in the Church of Scotland and voluntaries from the United Free Church. For the future of the Church that section of Article 3 had far-reaching consequences.

The stress on the importance of the territorial principle in the Articles Declaratory during the years leading up to reunion ended any likelihood that the social theology of the reunited Church would include an understanding of the Kingdom of God that involved the Church's engagement with social, political and economic issues. It ensured that for a considerable length of time, the Church of Scotland would primarily be concerned with the building up of congregations within the local parish.

Both Churches had believed in a territorial ministry. Thomas Chalmers had left the Free Church the legacy of his schemes for working a local area in St John's in Glasgow and the West Port in Edinburgh. The state's refusal to regard ministers of the Chapels of Ease, which Thomas Chalmers championed the more effectively to deploy ministers in areas of need, was possibly the final straw that broke Chalmers' reluctance to support disruption. The Church of Scotland's ministry was mainly sustained by the teinds paid by local landowners for the maintenance of the parish church and its ordained minister. There were, however, differences in the two Churches' attitudes towards territorial ministry. The basic unit for ministry and mission in the Church of Scotland was the parish, which for a long time after the Reformation had a civil as well as a religious connotation in that the Church was responsible for education and the care of the poor. Although these functions were gradually taken over by local government, the parish continued to be used as the basic unit of civil administration. There was a strong element in the United Free Church, going back to the secessions of the eighteenth century, that regarded the parish church with its civic duties as an inextricable part of the establishment. In the United Free Church the basic unit for ministry and mission was the presbytery, which was originally intended to oversee the local parishes. The Church of Scotland view was that using the presbytery as the basic unit allowed ministers and congregations to follow a mobile population. An area of deprivation where religious commitment was slight might be abandoned to a mission station without a minister and yet the presbytery could still claim to be committed to the presbytery area as a whole.

When the Church of Scotland began to recover from the Disruption, it was under the leadership of Principal William Robertson of Edinburgh University, who insisted that only the Church of Scotland, as an established Church, could properly fulfil the obligations to the nation. Meanwhile, the Free Church gradually moved away from the famous claim of Thomas Chalmers that he was leaving a vitiated establishment but looked forward to returning to a pure one, and, especially after the union with the United Presbyterian Church in 1900, the United Free Church's ecclesiastical policy became much more voluntary, rejecting what it regarded as state connection and funding.

Douglas Murray has pointed out that, when the time came in 1925 to prepare to draw up a formal Basis and Plan of Union between the two Churches, there was a minority in the United Free Church that was convinced that even after seeking parliamentary approval for its claim to spiritual independence, the Church of Scotland was irredeemably established, and a minority in the Church of Scotland that believed that as a result of the parliament's upholding the principles of the Articles Declaratory, it was no longer established. In an attempt to minimise the size of any group in the United Free Church likely to refuse to enter the union, counsel's opinion was sought as to whether, as a result of the Acts passed by parliament in 1929 and 1925, the Church of Scotland was free of state control. Even when the opinion was given that the United Free Church's principle of spiritual independence would not be compromised by union with the Church of Scotland, an unconvinced, but smaller minority believed otherwise. There was also a Church of Scotland minority that believed that as a result of the Church of Scotland Acts, the Church was no different from any other Church in the land, and so could only be thought of as 'national' because of its size and not its relationship with the state. As Douglas Murray points out, however, a significant difference between the two minorities was that those in the Church of Scotland could not separate and continue as an established Church, whereas the minority in the United Free Church could refuse to join a united Church and still witness to the voluntary principle.[33]

A means had to be found whereby it could be shown that the united Church would not compromise the United Free Church's principles of equality and spiritual independence but yet would allow the Church of Scotland to be assured that its historic link to the nation continued. The description of the Church of Scotland as 'national' was a way of doing this; but to reassure the United Free Church critics, John White made clear that a Church was national not because it had been accorded special status but because it accepted national obligations, the principal one being the territorial ministry, which had been supported in the past by teinds and would now be supported by endowments provided as a result of the agreement reached with the landowners to pay a capital sum to be relieved of the obligation to pay teinds. White wrote,

> This territorial system made certain that there is no place in Scotland, in secluded parish, in crowded street or overcrowded slum in which there was not an ordained servant of the Church, whose business it was to care for the highest good of every man, woman and child.[34]

As the reunion movement became more likely to succeed, it became necessary to stress the territorial ministry as a unifying principle. In his 1925 moderatorial address White asked for efficiency so that the ministry to the whole of Scotland could be more effectively carried out. When eventually commending the Basis and Plan of Union, White said that when it had been sent to presbyteries for comment, the returns

> showed a very general desire – which was attended to – to have specific reference made in the Basis to the duty of the Church of Scotland undertaking the provision of religious ordinances and pastoral care coextensive with Scotland and adapted to the territorial distribution of the population. The conferring churches attach the greatest importance to this system and recognise the necessity of safeguarding its continuance in the united church ... The Church must make systematic provision by mapping

the country out into parishes or ecclesiastical districts for bringing the gospel to the doors of the entire population.[35]

And so the following year White was able to move the adoption of the Basis and Plan of Union and the Act uniting the two Churches, describing the territorial principle as one of 'the essential principles about which there could be no compromise'.[36] And Principal Martin, proposing that the United Free Church agree to the Basis and Plan of Union, said that

> in crowded cities and congested areas, there are masses of spiritual hungry, often socially angry, whose plight cried that they be recovered for the Kingdom and for the happier and fuller life which only the blessings of the Kingdom could give.[37]

Because of the acceptance of the territorial principle in the united Church, their cries would be met.

Those in the United Free Church who opposed the union did so partly because they believed that the social theology of the united Church would be less politically inclined and involved than they wanted. They belonged to that wing of the United Free Church that had lost the debate on social theology which took place in their General Assembly in the years leading up to the First World War. They opposed union with what they continued to regard as a state Church not only because they believed the union compromised the principle of spiritual independence but because they feared a state Church would not be willing to be critical of the action of the state and the policies of its governments. And if they listened to John White, they had good reason for thinking so when he said that one of the arguments for a national Church was that it would be able to make sure that its social theology was not biased in one particular direction, by which he meant in the direction of those who wanted to involve the Church more in political and economic issues.

It is difficult to escape the conclusion that the decision to promote the united Church as a national Church through the commitment to a territorial ministry was the triumph of hope over experience. Church leaders knew the parochial system was not working. In his sermon at the opening of the Synod of Glasgow and Ayr in 1887, Marshall Lang talked about the failure of the parochial system to realise its legitimate end. He referred to increases in population so rapid that the parochial system could not keep pace with them.[38] But when he gave his address as Moderator to the 1893 General Assembly he said that territorial or parochial economy was the best means of securing strengthening food for the masses and the Church had to safeguard it.[39] In 1885, Donald Macleod said that in most of the large cities the parochial system could hardly be said to exist,[40] but in 1895 in his moderatorial address he said that the loss of the endowed parochial system was too high a price to pay for Church union.[41] When Dr William Smith, minister of North Leith and Convener of the Church of Scotland's Endowment Committee, gave the third set of Baird Lectures on the subject of the Endowed Territorial Work, he extolled its virtues and insisted that it must continue, but pointed out that its theoretical excellence was undermined by presbyteries being too large to exercise oversight, by population movements too serious for the territorial system to cope with, and by ministers and Kirk Sessions refusing to provide information on which presbyteries could make decisions about resources.[42] The leadership of the Church of Scotland seems to have been in some state of collective denial about its territorial work, as if the inability of the large towns and cities to cope with the influx of population that had occurred since the Industrial Revolution was a minor problem with which a revamped system could cope and not an inescapable factor which would not be overcome or wished away.

The effect of this insistence on stressing the territorial system in the united Church was that the territorial parish and the work of the Christian community within it became the primary focus of Christian commitment. It would have been a revival of the idea of the 'godly commonwealth' ideal had it not been for the fact that people no longer lived and worked in the same place. As the Edinburgh theologian Ruth Page has pointed out, the nature of the Church changed dramatically when its base in congregations moved from where people both lived and worked to merely where people lived.[43] Building up the local congregation became the primary focus of the Church's mission. Conditions in society were secondary, and social criticism and theology were the poorer for a generation.

To see how true that was, it is necessary to peer briefly beyond the union of 1929 into the life of the united Church and what was known as the Forward Movement. After the euphoria of the reunion died down, the Church of Scotland was faced with the need to rethink its strategy completely. The Church of Scotland did what it was so often to do: instead of developing a new strategy it convinced itself the old one simply required to be restated and reinforced. It went back to the territorial parish and the local congregation as the focal point of renewal. The result was the Forward Movement, which invoked the language of the Kingdom of God but envisaged a return to the old parochial, territorial principle. One of the documents that the Movement produced said, with more confidence than accuracy, that as a result of the union of the Churches in 1929, 'Chalmers's territorial principle, cherished by the Church of Scotland ever since his day, was now for the first time capable of being thoroughly carried out'. The Articles Declaratory of the Constitution of the Church of Scotland, which were the necessary prelude to the United Free Church entering the union, explicitly commit the reunited Church to the advancement of the Kingdom of God, but, as the Forward Movement's optimistic statement quoted above goes on to make clear, what the advancement of the Kingdom of God meant for the organisers was 'not only the pastoral care of the people but the evangelisation of Scotland'.

The Forward Movement was launched at the first routine meeting of the General Assembly in May 1930. Over two hundred people, ministers and elders, were assigned to twelve commissions whose reports were collated and edited by the Revd J. W. Stevenson, a young minister and journalist who was later to be a distinguished editor of *Life and Work* and who edited a symposium examining the relationship between the Scottish Church and working people.[44] Most of the articles had already been published in the *Scots Observer* while Stevenson was its editor, and they are in the main unremarkable. It took a layman, Patrick Geddes, whose academic career included occupying the Chairs of Sociology in Bombay and of Botany at St Andrews, to see the Kingdom of God advancing beyond the Church's walls in terms Robert Flint would have recognised:

> Our small beginnings, day by day – whether of the churchman in his study, the scientist in his social observatory and laboratory, or the creative worker in his studio – are already full of promise that these can alike, and before long, come out into people's lives, and work together for good. Insofar as our small beginnings are of true leaven and of true seed our small beginnings are of Hope; and so what better age to live in?[45]

While Geddes looked forward to the people being the beneficiaries of contemporary advances, J. W. Stevenson was simply concerned to annex them to the Church. 'How is the everyday life of industry and commerce and art and the professions to be brought within the Christian fellowship?' he asked. He did, however, realise that 'man's confidence in the Church as a Christian fellowship pledged to seek the establishment of a Divine Kingdom here and now, has been shaken by her long and ominous silences in the great crises of the modern world'.

Stevenson collated the reports of the twelve commissions.[46] They were mainly concerned with the Church's internal affairs, beginning with the regulation of baptism, frequency of communion, the religious life of the Christian family. Another commission listed the evangelistic outreach made by the Church. A commission examining the Church's impact on society reported on 'centres of social effort' such as the Church's homes, but moved on to criticise intemperance, gambling and moral laxity, and in conclusion said that 'in its own mission as an instrument of the Kingdom of God the Church possesses a force sufficient to effect a creative and constructive use of leisure'.

The reports of the Forward Movement commissions devoted 80 pages to the organisation of the Church at home, and 129 pages to missionary work abroad, ending with this appeal:

> To every member of the Church is addressed the call to enter upon a more sincere and eager and wholehearted life and service, until all the resources of the Church are at God's disposal and our faith claims his resources in all their plenitude for the service of his son and of his Kingdom.

The Forward Movement held a congress in Glasgow in October 1931 to discuss the reports that Stevenson compiled. It was attended by 2,500 people. Twenty area meetings, each lasting about a week, were held with the title 'Missions of the Kingdom', but their main aim was the revival of the territorial ideal and the parish community. These meetings were intended to stimulate congregational interest in visiting the parish to increase Church membership, and also the current members' involvement with such organisations as groups for young people, local charities, work with the unemployed and Sunday Schools. S. J. Brown concludes:

> For all the careful planning, investment of money and mission activity, however, the Forward Movement proved a disappointment. It failed to arouse much zeal for the Church's national mission among a population which was increasingly suffering the effects of the world economic depression of the 1930s.

Brown goes on to explain that John White was not surprised at the movement's failure because he believed

> that economic depression was bound to hamper efforts to revive the Church, as religious revivals tended to occur only in times of relative prosperity and security. In short, he maintained, religious revival would only come with a national social and economic revival.[47]

The futures of Church and state were apparently bound together, but hardly in the relationship envisaged by those who had believed in the Kingdom of Christ upon earth.

Ian Henderson has written that George Macleod's ministry in Govan in the 1930s

> did a lot to set the pattern for the post 1929 Union Church of Scotland ministry. It was to be the parish ministry of the Auld Kirk, not the chaplaincy to a ministry of middle-class families of the United Free one.[48]

Only to the extent that the ministry of the reunited Church had a legal obligation to provide the ordinances of religion in every parish, and that its parish ministers were obliged to conduct funerals and perform marriages to all, whether or not there was a connection with the Church of Scotland, is Henderson's judgement accurate. In terms of the ethos of the reunited Church, the emphasis was on building up its congregations. Of course the intention was that the local congregation would become the agent of mission and social concern within the parish area, but in reality the Church as a focus for social activities and events became much more prominent. The popular song about 'the kirk soiree' was a very accurate image. The reluctance to deal with the number of congregations and church buildings that were duplicated across the country resulted in competition between congregations rather than the cooperative vision of the advancement of the Kingdom of God that John White and Alexander Martin had held out as the fruits of reunion. Further movements of population took place and members of congregations retained a connection with where they had once lived. The administrative centralisation that the United Free Church had institutionalised in the building in 1929 of its offices in Edinburgh's George Street became a feature of the united Church's strategy of building up the local congregation for mission; it was to become, however, not a facilitator of evangelical outreach and social concern but an instrument of administrative convenience. It took forty years before the Kingdom of God as it was once envisaged by Robert Flint again emerged as a significant item on the Kirk's agenda.

It is difficult to look back over the decline within the Presbyterian Churches of Robert Flint's attempt to insert some urgency and content to social theology without a sense of considerable disappointment. His views were and are open to criticism and there was an element of confusion in them. But he brought the Church's contribution to social criticism out of the self-centredness of the sanctuary and offered a model for a new form of engagement with society. A. C. Cheyne has written of the wartime Baillie Commission that there is some reason to think that it helped pave the way for a 'seismic shift' that took place in the social thinking of this country and produced the Beveridge Report and the National Health Service.[49] John Baillie's own antipathy towards the idea of progress, and its reflection in the reports of his Commission, are clear rejections of the basis of Robert Flint's theory of gradual historical and contemporary development towards the Kingdom of God. Flint equally deserves credit, however, for laying down a basis on which the Church could again regard the engagement with society and its secular agencies as an integral part of its mission.

The century separating Robert Burns in Paisley, who was to join the Free Church, from the reunion of the divided strands of Presbyterianism in 1929 saw social criticism and theology eclipsed by the urgent need of the reunited Church of Scotland to sustain the unsustainable number of congregations that it failed to address then, and is still failing to address today. The Church of Scotland in the years after 1929 insisted that energised and lively congregational life would advance the Kingdom of God, but it failed to demonstrate any meaningful connection between the two. Flint's passionate vision of the Kingdom of Christ on earth was abandoned for the platitudes about the Kingdom of God inherited from John White and the requirements of the reunion negotiations.

During the Second World War, the American theologian Reinhold Niebuhr contributed an article to *Life and Work* that could be seen as a commentary on the eclipse of social criticism in the inter-war years:

> Many a pulpit imagines that it has fulfilled the task of the Church in guiding the conscience of the state or the nation when it asserts that nations must do God's will and affirm that business must be conducted according to the golden rule. It is, of course, perfectly true that if all men and nations perfectly fulfilled the law of love, it would not be difficult to organise a world community of nations. It is also true that the complicated apparatus of the national government would be unnecessary, for each man would desire the advantage of his neighbour and not his own. Neither trade union nor legal restraints on the activities of trades unions would be necessary because employers and workers would live in the brotherhood of the Kingdom of God; but it is rather fatuous to reiterate that truth if that is all we have to say about the problem of the human community.[50]

NOTES

1. John White Papers, 'Assembly Sunday, 1917', sermon preached in the Barony Church, Glasgow, University of Glasgow.
2. Watson, David (1901) *The Scottish Christian Social Union and How it Came to be Formed* (Glasgow: David J. Clark), p. 15.
3. Brown, S. J. (1994) 'The social ideal of the Church of Scotland in the 1930s', in A. Morton (ed.) *God's Will in a Time of Crisis* (Edinburgh: CTPI), pp. 14–31.
4. 'Christian Social Union', John White Papers, New College Library, Edinburgh, Box 50.
5. Brown, S. J. (1991) 'Reform, reconstruction, reaction: the social vision of Scottish Presbyterianism c1830–c1930', *Scottish Journal of Theology*, vol. 44.
6. Muir, Augustus (1958) *John White* (London: Hodder and Stoughton), p. 169.
7. *Proceedings and Debates, 1919*, p. 218.
8. Paterson, William P. (1919) *Recent History and the Call to Brotherhood* (Edinburgh: William Blackwood & Sons).

9. Paterson, William P. and Watson, David (1919) *Social Evils and Problems* (Edinburgh: William Blackwood & Sons).
10. Ibid. p. 27.
11. Ibid. p. 8.
12. Ibid. p. 23.
13. Brown, S. J. (1919) '"A victory for God": the Scottish Presbyterian Churches and the General Strike of 1926', *Journal of Ecclesiastical History*, vol. 42, no. 4, pp. 596–617.
14. Ibid. pp. 596–617.
15. Smith, *Passive Obedience and Prophetic Protest*, p. 361.
16. John White Papers, New College Edinburgh, Box 50.
17. Ibid. Box 5.
18. *The Scotsman*, 29 May 1925.
19. Ibid. 19 May 1926.
20. Ibid. 29 May 1925.
21. Ibid. 26 May 1928.
22. Reith, George (ed.) (1921) *Proceedings and Debates of the United Free Church General Assembly* (Edinburgh: McNiven and Wallace), p. 216.
23. Reith, George (ed.) (1923) *Proceedings and Debates of the United Free Church General Assembly* (Edinburgh: McNiven and Wallace), p. 140.
24. Reith, George (ed.) (1924) *Proceedings and Debates of the United Free Church General Assembly* (Edinburgh: McNiven and Wallace), p. 264.
25. Reith, George (ed.) (1926) *Proceedings and Debates of the United Free Church General Assembly* (Edinburgh: McNiven and Wallace), p. 212.
26. Reith, George (ed.) (1927) *Proceedings and Debates of the United Free Church General Assembly* (Edinburgh: McNiven and Wallace), p. 153.
27. Reith, George (ed.) (1922) *Proceedings and Debates of the United Free Church General Assembly* (Edinburgh: McNiven and Wallace), p. 46.
28. Ibid. p. 46.
29. Reith, George (ed.) (1919) *Proceedings and Debates of the United Free Church General Assembly* (Edinburgh: McNiven and Wallace), p. 45.
30. Ibid. p. 45.
31. Reith, George (ed.) (1920) *Proceedings and Debates of the United Free Church General Assembly* (Edinburgh: McNiven and Wallace), p. 45.
32. Reith, George (ed.) (1924) *Proceedings and Debates of the United Free Church General Assembly* (Edinburgh: McNiven and Wallace), p. 165.
33. Murray, Douglas (2000) *Rebuilding the Kirk* (Edinburgh: Scottish Academic Press), p. 205ff.
34. John White Papers, 'The territorial ministry', New College Edinburgh, Box 99.
35. Ibid.
36. *The Scotsman*, 26 May 1928.
37. Ibid.
38. Lang, *They Need not Depart*, p. 12.

39. Lang, John M. (1893), *The Church and the People* (Edinburgh: William Blackwood & Sons), p. 35.

40. Macleod, Donald (1886) 'The parochial system', *The Church and the People, St Giles' Lectures, 6th Series* (Edinburgh: McNiven and Wallace), p. 109ff.

41. Macleod, Donald (1895) *Lines of Progress* (Edinburgh: William Blackwood & Sons), p. 17ff.

42. Smith, William (1875) *Endowed Territorial Work* (Glasgow: William Blackwood & Sons), available, along with all the Baird Lectures, at www.clydeserve/bairdtrust/node/7

43. Page, Ruth (2000) *God with us; Synergy in the Church* (London: SCM Press), p. 96.

44. Stevenson, John W. (1930) *The Healing of the Nation* (Edinburgh: T. & T. Clark).

45. Ibid.

46. Stevenson, John W. (1931) *The Call to the Church* (Edinburgh: Church of Scotland Publications Committee).

47. Brown (1994) 'The social ideal of the Church of Scotland'.

48. Henderson, Ian (1969) *Scotland: Kirk And People* (London: Lutterworth Press), p. 47.

49. Cheyne, A. C. (1999) *Studies in Church History* (Edinburgh: T. & T. Clark), p. 251.

50. Niebuhr, Reinhold (1943) 'Justice in the Church and among the Nations', *Life and Work*, August 1943, pp. 117–18.

Bibliography

OFFICIAL CHURCH RECORDS

Lamb, John A. (1956) *The Fasti of the United Free Church of Scotland, 1900–1929* (Edinburgh: Oliver and Boyd).

Minutes of the Presbytery of Glasgow, 1877–87, CH2/171/24.

Minutes of the Presbytery of Glasgow, 1888–1900, CH2/171/25.

Minutes of the Presbytery of Paisley, 1823–36, CH2/294/14.

Minutes of the Presbytery of Paisley, 1836–43, CH2/294/15.

Minutes of the United Free Church Presbytery of Glasgow, CH3/146/44.

Official Report of Proceedings of the First Church Congress, 1899 (Edinburgh: J. Gardner Hitt).

Paisley Abbey Kirk Session Weekday Minute Book, 1829–53, National Archive of Scotland, CH2/490/51.

Proceedings and Debates of the General Assembly of the Free Church of Scotland, 1843–1900 (Edinburgh: Free Church of Scotland).

Proceedings and Debates of the United Free Church of Scotland, 1904–29 (Edinburgh: United Free Church of Scotland).

Report of Commission on the Housing of the Poor in relation to their Social Conditions, 1891 (Glasgow: Presbytery of Glasgow).

Reports of the Schemes of the Church of Scotland, 1866–1914 (Edinburgh: Church of Scotland).

Reports to the General Assembly of the United Free Church of Scotland, 1904–29 (Edinburgh: United Free Church of Scotland).

Scott, Hew (ed.) (1916–28) *Fasti Ecclesiae Scoticanae*, vols 1–9 (Edinburgh: Oliver and Boyd).

Scottish Church Society Conferences, 1st Series, 1894 (Edinburgh: James McLehose & Sons).

The Churches' Task in Social Reform, Report of the Proceedings of the United Free Church Congress on Social Problems, November 1911 (Edinburgh: Oliphant, Anderson and Ferrier).

GOVERNMENT AND MUNICIPAL REPORTS

Municipal Commission on the Housing of the Poor (1904), Corporation of Glasgow.

Municipal Glasgow, Its Evolution and Enterprises (1914), Corporation of Glasgow.

PRIMARY SOURCES

Brewster, Patrick, Scrapbook.

Brewster, Patrick (1833) *Heroism of the Christian Spirit* (Edinburgh: A. & C. Black).

Brewster, Patrick (1835) *The Claims of the Church of Scotland on the Support and Affection of the People* (Paisley: n.p.).

Brewster, Patrick (1836) *An Essay on Passive Obedience* (Paisley: Alexander Gardner).

Brewster, Patrick (1842) *The Seven Chartist and Military Discourses Ordered by the General Assembly to be Libelled by the Presbytery of Paisley* (Glasgow: Forward).

Brewster, Patrick (1843) *The Legal Rights of the Poor of Scotland Vindicated* (Paisley: published by the author).

Buchanan, Robert (1850) *The Schoolmaster in the Wynds* (Glasgow: Blackie & Son).

Buchanan, Robert (1851) *The Spiritual Destitution of the Masses in Glasgow* (Glasgow: Blackie & Son).

Buchanan, Robert (1851) *A Second Appeal on the Spiritual Destitution of the Masses in Glasgow* (Glasgow: Blackie & Son).

Burns, Robert (1819) *Historical Dissertations on the Law and Practice of Great Britain and particularly of Scotland with regard to the Poor* (Edinburgh: Peter Hill).

Burns, Robert (1841) *A Plea for the Poor of Scotland, Two Lectures* (Paisley: Alexander Gardner).

Burns, Robert (1842) *Christian Patriotism in Times of Distress* (Paisley: Alexander Gardner).

Clow, William M. (1911) *The Secret of the Lord* (London: Hodder and Stoughton).

Clow, William M. (1913) *Christ in the Social Order* (London: Hodder and Stoughton).

Flint, Robert, Papers, Edinburgh University Library, Boxes H57, Gen 631–88.

Flint, Robert, Papers, New College Library, Edinburgh, MSS FLI 1–3.

Flint, Robert (1865) *Christ's Kingdom upon Earth* (Edinburgh: William Blackwood & Sons).

Flint, Robert (1883) 'Norman Macleod', *Scottish Divines, St Giles' Lectures, 3rd series* (Edinburgh: McNiven and Wallace).

Flint, Robert (1895) *Socialism* (London: Isbister & Co.).

Flint, Robert (1899) *Sermons and Addresses* (Edinburgh: William Blackwood & Sons).

Flint, Robert (1903) *Agnosticism* (New York: Charles Scribner's Sons).

Flint, Robert (1905) *On Theological, Biblical and Other Subjects* (Edinburgh: William Blackwood & Sons).

Lang, John Marshall (1887) *They Need not Depart* (Glasgow: Boyce & Son).

Lang, John Marshall (1902) *The Church and its Social Mission* (Edinburgh: William Blackwood & Sons).

Macleod, Donald (ed.) (1872–1916) *Good Words* (London: Isbister & Co.).

Macleod, Donald (1893) *Christ and Society* (London: Isbister & Co.).

Macleod, Donald (1886) 'The parochial system', *The Church and the People, St Giles' Lectures, 6th Series* (Edinburgh: McNiven and Wallace).

Macleod, Donald (1888) *Non-Church-Going and the Housing of the Poor* (Glasgow: William Blackwood & Sons).

Macleod, Norman (1862) *Parish Papers* (London: Alexander Strahan & Co.).

Macleod, Norman (1866) 'Improving the condition of the poor', *Good Words* (London: Alexander Strahan & Co.).

Macleod, Norman (1872) 'God's will be done', *Good Words* (London: Alexander Strahan & Co.).

Matheson, A. Scott (1890) *The Gospel and Modern Substitutes* (Edinburgh: Oliphant, Anderson and Ferrier).

Matheson, A. Scott (1893) *The Church and Social Problems* (Edinburgh: Oliphant, Anderson and Ferrier).

Matheson, A. Scott (1910) *The City of Man* (London: T. Fisher Unwin).

Report of a Soiree in Honour of the Rev. Patrick Brewster, November 12, 1838 (Paisley: Caldwell & Son).

Watson, David (1901) *Child Life in Cities* (Glasgow: Begg, Kennedy and Elder).

Watson, David (1905) *Perfect Manhood* (London: Hodder and Stoughton).

Watson, David (1908) *Social Problems and the Church's Duty* (Edinburgh: R. & R. Clark).

Watson, David (1911) *Social Advance: Its Meaning, Message and Goal* (London: Hodder and Stoughton).

Watson, David (1919) *The Social Expression of Christianity* (London: Hodder and Stoughton).

Watson, David (1936) *Chords of Memory* (Edinburgh: William Blackwood & Sons).

UNPUBLISHED PRIMARY SOURCES

Flint Papers, Edinburgh University Library; New College Library, Edinburgh.

White Papers, New College Library, Edinburgh; Glasgow University Library.

NEWSPAPERS AND PERIODICALS

Glasgow Herald

Life and Work

Paisley Advertiser
Renfrewshire Advertiser
The Bailie
The Scotsman

BOOKS PUBLISHED BEFORE 1914

Bruce, Alexander B. (1886) *The Miraculous Elements in the Gospels* (London: Hodder and Stoughton).

Bruce, Alexander B. (1890) *The Kingdom of God*, 3rd edn (Edinburgh: T. & T. Clark).

Burns, Robert F. (1871) *The Life and Times of the Rev. Robert Burns, DD* (Toronto: J. Campbell).

Candlish, James (1884) *The Kingdom of God* (Edinburgh: T. & T. Clark).

Cooper, James (1895) *Disestablishment and Disendowment Contrary to Holy Scripture* (Aberdeen: John Rae Smith).

Cooper, James (1895) *The Revival of Church Principles in the Church of Scotland* (Oxford: Mowbray & Co.).

Cooper, James (1898) *The Church Catholic and National* (Glasgow: James McLehose & Sons).

Cooper, James (1902) *A United Church for the British Empire* (Forres: n.p.).

Drummond, Robert J. (1900) *The Relation of the Apostolic Teaching to the Teaching of Christ* (Edinburgh: T. & T. Clark).

Engels, Friedrich (1936) *Conditions of the Working Class in England* (London: Allen and Unwin).

MacCall, D. (1867) *Among the Masses* or *The Work in the Wynds* (Glasgow: James McLehose & Sons).

Macleod, Donald (1876) *Memoir of Norman Macleod, DD*, 2 vols (New York: Scribner, Armstrong & Co.).

Ross, John M. E. (1905) *William Ross of Cowcaddens* (London: Hodder and Stoughton).

Thomson, James (1905) *A History of St Andrew's Parish* (Glasgow: Robert Anderson).

Walker, Norman L. (1877) *Robert Buchanan, An Ecclesiastical Biography* (London: Thomas Nelson).

Walker, Norman L. (1895) *Chapters from the History of the Free Church of Scotland* (Edinburgh: Moray Press).

Westcott, Brooke F. (1887) *The Social Aspects of Christianity* (London: Macmillan & Co.).

BOOKS PUBLISHED SINCE 1914

Aspinwall, Bernard (1984) *Portable Utopia: Glasgow and the United States 1820–1920* (Aberdeen: Aberdeen University Press).

Barbour, Robin S. (1993) *The Kingdom of God and Human Society* (Edinburgh: T. & T. Clark).

Brown, Callum G. (1987) *Social History of Religion in Scotland since 1730* (Edinburgh: Edinburgh University Press).

Brown, Callum G. (1997) *Religion and Society in Scotland since 1707* (Edinburgh: Edinburgh University Press).

Brown, Callum G. (2001) *The Death of Christian Britain* (London: Routledge).

Brown, S. J. (1982) *Thomas Chalmers and the Godly Commonwealth in Scotland* (Oxford: Oxford University Press).

Brown, S. J. (2008) *Providence and Empire* (Harlow: Pearson Longman).

Cameron, Nigel (ed.) (1993) *Dictionary of Scottish Church History and Theology* (Edinburgh: T. & T. Clark).

Chadwick, Owen (1970) *The Victorian Church*, 2 vols (London: A. & C. Black).

Checkland, Olive and Checkland, Sydney (1989) *Industry and Ethos, Scotland 1832–1914* (Edinburgh: Edinburgh University Press).

Checkland, Sydney (1977) *The Upas Tree* (Glasgow: University of Glasgow Press).

Cheyne, A. C. (1983) *The Transforming of the Kirk* (Edinburgh: Saint Andrew Press).

Cheyne, A. C. (ed.) (1985) *The Practical and the Pious* (Edinburgh: Saint Andrew Press).

Davies, W. Merlin. (1964) *An Introduction to F. D. Maurice's Theology* (London: SPCK).

Devine, T. C. (1999) *The Scottish Nation, 1700–2000* (London: Penguin Press).

Drummond, Andrew L. and Bulloch, James B. P. (1978) *The Church in Late Victorian Scotland* (Edinburgh: Saint Andrew Press).

Drummond, R. J. (1951) *Lest we Forget, Reminiscences of a Nonagenarian* (Edinburgh: Ettrick Press).

Engels, Friedrich (1936) *Conditions of the Working Class in England* (London: Allen and Unwin).

Ferguson, T. (1948) *The Dawn of Scottish Social Welfare* (London: Thomas Nelson).

Ferguson, T. (1958) *Scottish Social Welfare, 1864–1914* (Edinburgh: E. & S. Livingstone).

Fleming, J. R. (1927) *The Church in Scotland, 1843–1874* (Edinburgh: T. & T. Clark).

Fleming, J. R. (1933) *The Church in Scotland, 1875–1929* (Edinburgh: T. & T. Clark).

Fraser W. Hamish (2010) *Chartism in Scotland* (Pontypool: Merlin Press).

Hick, John (1968) *Evil and the God of Love* (London: Macmillan & Co).

Hoppen, K. Theodore (1998) *The Mid-Victorian Generation, 1846–1886* (Oxford: Oxford University Press).

Knox, William W. (1999) *Industrial Nation* (Edinburgh: Edinburgh University Press).

Lundstrom, Gosta (1963) (trans. J. Bulman) *The Kingdom of God in the Teaching of Jesus* (London: Oliver and Boyd).

Macdonald, Lesley (2000) *A Unique and Glorious Mission: Women and Presbyterianism in Scotland 1830–1930* (Edinburgh: John Donald).

MacMillan, Donald (1914) *The Life of Robert Flint* (London: Hodder and Stoughton).

McCaffrey, John (1998) *Scotland in the Nineteenth Century* (London: Macmillan Press).

McKinstry, Leo (2006) *Rosebery: A Statesman in Turmoil* (London: John Murray).

Mechie, Stewart (1960) *The Church and Scottish Social Development, 1780–1870* (London: Oxford University Press).

Murray, Douglas. M. (2000) *Rebuilding the Kirk* (Edinburgh: Scottish Academic Press).

Niebuhr, H. Richard (1959) *The Kingdom of God in America* (New York: Harper and Row).

Paterson, William P. (1919) *Recent History and the Call to Brotherhood* (Edinburgh: William Blackwood & Sons).

Paterson, William P. and Watson, David (1919) *Social Evils and Problems* (Edinburgh: William Blackwood & Sons).

Robbins, Keith (2008) *England, Ireland, Scotland, Wales: The Christian Church 1900–2000* (Oxford: Oxford University Press).

Scotland, James (1969) *The History of Scottish Education*, vol. 2 (London: University of London Press).

Sell, Alan P. F. (1987) *Defending and Declaring the Faith, Some Scottish Examples 1860–1920* (Exeter: Paternoster Press).

Smith, Donald C. (1987) *Passive Obedience and Prophetic Protest* (New York: Peter Lang).

Smith, Sydney (1926) *Donald Macleod of Glasgow* (London: James Clarke & Co.).

Storrar, William (1990) *Scottish Identity* (Edinburgh: The Handsel Press).

Vidler, Alec R. (1966) *F. D. Maurice and Company* (London: SCM).

Wilson, Alexander (1970) *The Chartist Movement in Scotland* (Manchester: Manchester University Press).

Wright, Leslie C. (1953) *Scottish Chartism* (Edinburgh: Oliver and Boyd).

PAMPHLETS AND ARTICLES IN PERIODICALS

Aiton, J. (1859) *A Tribute to the Memory of the Poor Man's Champion* (Glasgow: Thomas Murray & Son).

Brown, Callum G. (1996) '"To be aglow with civic ardours": the "Godly

Commonwealth" in Glasgow, 1843–1914', *Records of the Scottish Church History Society*, vol. XXVI.

Brown, S. J. (1991) 'Reform, reconstruction, reaction: the social vision of Scottish Presbyterianism c1830–c1930', *Scottish Journey of Theology*, vol. 44.

Brown, S. J. (1994) 'The social ideal of the Church of Scotland in the 1930s', in A. Morton (ed.) *God's Will in a Time of Crisis* (Edinburgh: CTPI).

Brown, S. J. (1994) '"A victory for God": The Scottish Presbyterian Churches and the General Strike of 1926', *Journal of Ecclesiastical History*, vol. 42, no. 4.

Brown, S. J. (2006) 'Watson, David (1859–1943)', in Lawrence Goldman (ed.), *Oxford Dictionary of National Biography*, available at http:/www.oxford dnb.com/view/article/92318, accessed 26 December 2006.

Hillis, Peter (1981) 'Presbyterianism and social class in mid-nineteenth century Glasgow: a study of nine churches', *Journal of Ecclesiastical History*, vol. 32, no. 1.

Hillis, Peter (1992) 'Towards a new social theology; the contribution of Norman Macleod', *Records of the Scottish Church History Society*, vol. XXIV.

Leneman, L. (1992) 'The Scottish churches and "Votes for Woman"', *Records of the Scottish Church History Society*, vol. XXIV.

Marwick, W. H. (1953) 'Social heretics in the Scottish churches', *Records of the Scottish Church History Society*, vol. XI.

Withrington, Donald J. (1972) 'Non-churchgoing, c1750–c1850, a preliminary study', *Records of the Scottish Church History Society*, vol. XVII.

Withrington, Donald J. (1977) 'The churches in Scotland, c1870–c1900: towards a new social conscience', *Records of the Scottish Church History Society*, vol. XIX.

PHD THESES

Bishop, D. H. (1953) *Church and Society, A Study of the Social Work and Thought of James Begg DD (1808–1883), A. H. Charteris DD, LLD (1835–1908) and David Watson DD (1859–1943)* (unpublished doctoral thesis, University of Edinburgh).

Campbell, K. A. (1999) *The Free Church of Scotland and the Territorial Ideal, 1843–1900* (unpublished doctoral thesis, University of Edinburgh).

Obitts, S. R. (1962) *The Theology of Robert Flint* (unpublished doctoral thesis, University of Edinburgh).

Index